Rails

Pocket Reference

Rails
Pocket Reference

Eric Berry

Beijing · Cambridge · Farnham · Köln · Sebastopol · Taipei · Tokyo

Rails Pocket Reference
by Eric Berry

Copyright © 2008 Eric Berry. All rights reserved.
Printed in Canada.

Published by O'Reilly Media, Inc., 1005 Gravenstein Highway North, Sebastopol, CA 95472.

O'Reilly books may be purchased for educational, business, or sales promotional use. Online editions are also available for most titles (*http://safari .oreilly.com*). For more information, contact our corporate/institutional sales department: 800-998-9938 or *corporate@oreilly.com*.

Editor: Simon St.Laurent
Copy Editor: Katie Nopper DePasquale
Production Editor: Loranah Dimant
Proofreader: Loranah Dimant
Indexer: Joe Wizda
Cover Designer: Karen Montgomery
Interior Designer: David Futato
Illustrator: Jessamyn Read

Printing History:

September 2008:   First Edition.

ISBN: 978-0-596-52070-0

[TM]

1221067154

Contents

Preface

Ruby on Rails (RoR) is a web application framework written in Ruby (*http://www.ruby-lang.org*) that allows programmers like you to create database-backed web applications with incredible speed and simplicity. Ruby on Rails was written by David Heinemeier Hanson (DHH) who, while working for 37signals.com, wrote a collaboration tool called Basecamp (*http://www.basecamphq.com*). While extracting code from Basecamp for use in another application, DHH decided to create Rails and offer it as an open source project in July 2004. Rails uses the Model-View-Controller (MVC) architecture, which separates data (the model) from the interface (view) by means of a controller (for accessing data and business logic). For more information, visit *http://www.rubyonrails.org*.

Conventions Used in This Book

Italic

> Indicates new terms, URLs, email addresses, filenames, and file extensions.

`Constant width`

> Used for program listings, as well as within paragraphs to refer to program elements, such as variable or function names, options, databases, data types, environment variables, statements, and keywords.

`Constant width bold`

> Shows commands or other text that should be typed literally by the user.

`Constant width italic`

> Shows text that should be replaced with user-supplied values or with values determined by context.

Using Code Examples

This book is here to help you get your job done. In general, you may use the code in this book in your programs and documentation. You do not need to contact us for permission unless you're reproducing a significant portion of the code. For example, writing a program that uses several chunks of code from this book does not require permission. Selling or distributing a CD-ROM of examples from O'Reilly books does require permission. Answering a question by citing this book and quoting example code does not require permission. Incorporating a significant amount of example code from this book into your product's documentation does require permission.

We appreciate, but do not require, attribution. An attribution usually includes the title, author, publisher, and ISBN. For example: "*Rails Pocket Reference* by Eric Berry. Copyright 2008 Eric Berry, 978-0-596-52070-0."

If you feel your use of code examples falls outside fair use or the permission given above, feel free to contact us at *permissions@oreilly.com*.

Safari® Books Online

When you see a Safari® Books Online icon on the cover of your favorite technology book, that means the book is available online through the O'Reilly Network Safari Bookshelf.

Safari offers a solution that's better than e-books. It's a virtual library that lets you easily search thousands of top tech books, cut and paste code samples, download chapters, and find quick answers when you need the most accurate, current information. Try it for free at *http://safari.oreilly.com*.

How to Contact Us

Please address comments and questions concerning this book to the publisher:

> O'Reilly Media, Inc.
> 1005 Gravenstein Highway North
> Sebastopol, CA 95472
> 800-998-9938 (in the United States or Canada)
> 707-829-0515 (international or local)
> 707-829-0104 (fax)

We have a web page for this book, where we list errata, examples, and any additional information. You can access this page at:

> *http://www.oreilly.com/catalog/9780596520700*

To comment or ask technical questions about this book, send email to:

bookquestions@oreilly.com

For more information about our books, conferences, Resource Centers, and the O'Reilly Network, see our website at:

http://www.oreilly.com

Acknowledgments

This book is dedicated to all the Rails contributors and bloggers out there who are helping develop the best and most enjoyable framework ever made. I want to thank Ryan Bates for his invaluable Railscasts (railscasts.com), which has served as my personal tutor over the last year. I want to thank Gregg Pollack (*http://www.railsenvy.com*) for helping me take the material in this book to the next level. I would like to thank Ryan Daigle (*https://www/ryandaigle.com*), who always keeps the Rails community up-to-date on the latest and greatest pertaining to Rails and also provided me with excellent material and examples. I would like to thank all of those who have written technical books in the Ruby/Rails field. I now know it's much more difficult than I had imagined. Props! I would like to thank Simon St.Laurent for giving a new writer a chance when there were so many more experienced writers available. I would also like to thank Loranah Dimant for her keen eye and expert advice on preparing this book for publishing.

I would like to thank my beautiful wife, Aubree, for allowing me to work late nights and weekends on the book. Thanks, cutie!

Most of all, I would like to thank Michael Fitzgerald. You are the reason I was able to write this book in the first place. You have been an incredible inspiration to me, an excellent teacher, and a great friend. Thank you.

Rails Pocket Reference

About Rails Pocket Reference

I have been using Ruby on Rails for almost a year and a half now, which is not long compared to many of my colleagues. As my passion for the framework and language grew, so did my appetite for more knowledge. Now that I own about 12 books on Ruby on Rails and Ruby, I find that there is a true need for a pocket reference guide to Ruby on Rails.

This book does not contain new information that is not easily accessible online or in printed books. It is not meant to "shed new light" on the language or framework. It is merely my attempt to collect as much useful information as possible that a typical Rails developer like myself might find helpful on a daily basis. A large portion of the book contains actual Rails documentation, as provided by the Rails community, along with annotations and examples from myself and others.

Getting Started

To see whether Rails is running on your computer, type the following at a shell or command prompt:

```
rails --version
```

An affirmative response would look similar to this (example from Rails 2.1.0 running on Mac OS X):

```
Rails 2.1.0
```

RubyGems

RubyGems is a package utility for Ruby (*http://rubygems.ruby forge.org*). It was written by Jim Weirich (*http://onestepback .org*). It installs Ruby software packages like Rails and keeps them up-to-date. It is quite easy to learn and use, even easier than tools like the Unix/Linux tar utility (*http://www.gnu.org/ software/tar*) or Java's jar utility (*http://java.sun.com/j2se/1.5.0/ docs/tooldocs/windows/jar.html*).

For more information, read the RubyGems documentation at *http://docs.rubygems.org*. The RubyGems User Guide (*http:// docs.rubygems.org/read/book/1*) gives you most everything you need to know about using RubyGems. A command reference is also available (*http://docs.rubygems.org/read/book/2*).

Installing Rails with RubyGems

RubyGems is installed with Ruby, but if you want more information, go to Chapter 3 of the RubyGems User Guide for complete installation instructions (*http://rubygems.org/read/ chapter/3*).

To see which version of RubyGems is installed, type:

```
gem --version
```

To get help with RubyGems, you can try:

```
gem --help
```

To view a list of commands for RubyGems, type:

```
gem help commands
```

To list example commands with descriptions, type:

```
gem help examples
```

To view help on a specific command, type:

`gem help [command]`

To install or update Rails (**sudo** requires a root password), type:

`sudo gem install rails`

Using Instant Rails on Windows

Instant Rails is a Windows-based solution for running Ruby on Rails with Apache and MySQL. With Instant Rails, you can easily configure your Rails root folder and run it. There is no need for system environment modifications.

To install Instant Rails and create an application called myapp, do the following:

1. Download and unzip Instant Rails at *http://rubyforge .org/projects/instantrails*.

2. Make sure there are no space characters in the installation path, and then start *InstallRails.exe*.

3. Instant Rails will detect that it is being started from a new directory and ask if you want to have it regenerate the configuration files. Click OK.

4. Click on the I button to drop down the main menu and select Rails Applications → Manage Rails Applications....

5. In the editor that pops up, click the button Create New Rails App....

6. A console will open. Type **rails myapp**.

7. Now close the Rails Configuration window and reopen it by following step 4.

8. You will now see *myapp* in the Rails Applications list. Click the checkbox next to it and then click "Start with Mongrel."

9. Open a browser and go to *http://127.0.0.1:3000*.

10. Welcome aboard!

Gem Dependencies

Gem dependencies were added in Rails 2.1. This means required gems can now be specified in the *config/environment.rb* file and will automatically load when the application is started. For example:

```
Rails::Initializer.run do |config|

  # Specify gems that this application depends on.
  # They can then be installed with "rake gems:install" on new
installations.
  config.gem "bj"
  config.gem "hpricot", :version => '0.6',
                        :source => "http://code.whytheluckystiff.net"
  config.gem "aws-s3", :lib => "aws/s3"
  ...
end
```

Along with this, there is now a `rake` task that will install all the referenced `config.gems` on your target system:

```
rake gems:install
```

If you want to pull these gems into your application source, you can do so with the `rake gems:unpack` task:

```
# Unpack all gems to vendor/gems
rake gems:unpack
```

You can also unpack individual gems:

```
# Unpack only the hpricot gem to vendor/gems
rake gems:unpack GEM=aws-s3
```

This will unpack the gem into the *vendor/gems/aws-s3-x.x.x* directory, which is automatically searched as part of the `config.gem` startup.

To build gems that have native extensions, you can use the `rake gems:build` task:

```
rake gems:build

# Or build a specific gem
rake gems:build GEM=aws-s3
```

Rails Commands and Configuration

Once Rails is installed, the `rails` command can be used to generate new Rails applications with a default directory structure and configuration at the path you specify.

To create a Rails application called myapp, type:

```
rails myapp
```

Once this is run, you will see a list of directories and files displayed that were generated by the command. This is your Rails application, with myapp being the base folder, or RAILS ROOT.

Usage and Options

For help with the `rails` command, type:

```
rails --help
```

Usage

```
rails [/path/to/your/appname] [options]
```

Options

`r, ruby=path`
: Path to the Ruby binary of your choice

`-d, --database=name`
: Preconfigured for a selected database (e.g., `mysql`, `oracle`, `postgresql`, `sqlite2`, `sqlite3`)

`-f, --freeze`
: Freezes Rails in vendor/rails from the gems generating the skeleton

`-v, --version`
: Shows the Rails version number and quits

`-p, --pretend`
: Runs but does not make any changes

`--force`
: Overwrites files that already exist

-s, --skip
> Skips files that already exist

-q, --quiet
> Suppresses normal output

-t, --backtrace
> Debugging; shows backtrace on errors

-c, --svn
> Modifies files with subversion (svn must be in path)

Rails File Structure

After generating a Rails application, a default directory and file structure is created. See Table 1-1.

Table 1-1. Rails file structure

Path	Description
app	Holds all the code that's specific to this particular application.
app/controllers	Holds controllers that should be named like *users_controller.rb* for automated URL mapping. All controllers should descend from ApplicationController, which itself descends from ActionController::Base.
app/models	Holds models that should be named, like *product.rb*. Most models will descend from ActiveRecord::Base.
app/views	Holds the template files for the view that should be named, like *users/index.html.erb* for the UsersController index action. All views use eRuby syntax.
app/views/layouts	Holds the template files for layouts to be used with views. This models the common header/footer method of wrapping views. In your views, define a layout using the layout *:default*, and create a file named *default.html.erb*. Inside *default.html.erb*, call <%= yield %> to render the view using this layout.
app/helpers	Holds view helpers that should be named, like *users_helper.rb*. These are generated for you automatically when using script/generate for controllers. Helpers can be used to wrap functionality for your views into methods.

Path	Description
config	Configuration files for the Rails environment, the routing map, the database, and other dependencies.
db	Contains the database schema in *schema.rb.db/migrate*; contains all the sequences of migrations for your schema.
doc	This directory is where your application documentation will be stored when generated using `rake doc:app`.
lib	Application-specific libraries. Basically, any kind of custom code that doesn't belong under controllers, models, or helpers. This directory is in the load path.
public	The directory available for the web server. Contains subdirectories for images, stylesheets, and JavaScripts. Also contains the dispatchers and the default HTML files. This should be set as the DOCUMENT ROOT of your web server.
script	Helper scripts for automation and generation.
test	Unit and functional tests, along with fixtures. When using the script/generate scripts, template test files will be generated for you and placed in this directory.
vendor	External libraries that the application depends on. Also includes the plugins subdirectory. This directory is in the load path.

Configuring Rails

Every Rails application relies on its configuration files to specify how the application will work. These files are found in the *config* folder:

boot.rb
> Rails bootloader file. Typically, this file does not need to be modified.

routes.rb
> Configuration file in which routes are specified.

environment.rb
> General configuration settings for the Rails application.

environments/development.rb
> Configuration specific to the development environment.

environments/test.rb
> Configuration specific to the test environment.

environments/production.rb
> Configuration specific to the production environment.

database.yml
> Configures your database connection.

initializers/inflections.rb
> Adds new inflection rules to the application (i.e., plural, singular, irregular, uncountable).

initializers/mime_types.rb
> Adds new mime types for use in `respond_to` blocks (i.e., rtf or iPhone).

initializers/new_rails_defaults.rb
> These settings change the behavior of Rails 2 apps and will be defaults for Rails 3. *This file will be deprecated in Rails 3.*

For more information on routes, environments, and database configuration, see the appropriate sections in this book.

Scripts

Rails comes with helper scripts for automation and code generation. Using these scripts, developers can build applications quickly but retain control over generated content.

script/about

Displays information about your application's environment:

```
Ruby version            1.8.6 (universal-darwin9.0)
RubyGems version        1.1.1
Rails version           2.1.0
Active Record version   2.1.0
Action Pack version     2.1.0
Active Resource version 2.1.0
Action Mailer version   2.1.0
Active Support version  2.1.0
Application root         /Users/berry/Sites/myapp
Environment             development
```

```
Database adapter          sqlite3
Database schema version   2
```

script/console

The console gives you access to your Rails environment, where you can interact with the domain model. Here you'll have all parts of the application configured, just like it is when the application is running. You can inspect domain models, change values, and save to the database.

Start the console with the console script:

`./script/console`

Starting the console without any arguments will run the console using the development environment.

To exit the console, type:

`quit` or `exit`

With the later version of Rails, you can reload your models and controllers with the following command:

`reload!`

To reset your application, type:

`Dispatcher.reset_application!`

Usage

`./script/console [environment] [options]`

Options

`-s, --sandbox`
    Rolls back database modifications on exit

`--irb=[irb]`
    Invokes a different *irb*

script/destroy

This script will destroy all files created by the corresponding script/generate command. For instance, script/destroy migration CreatePost will delete the appropriate *###_create_post.rb* file in *db/migrate*, while script/destroy scaffold Post will delete the post controller and views, post model and migration, all associated tests, and the map.resources :posts line in *config/routes.rb*.

Usage

```
./script/destroy generator [options] [args]
```

Example

```
./script/destroy controller Products

       rm  app/helpers/products_helper.rb
       rm  test/functional/products_controller_test.rb
       rm  app/controllers/products_controller.rb
    rmdir  test/functional
 notempty  test
    rmdir  app/views/products
 notempty  app/views
 notempty  app
 notempty  app/helpers
 notempty  app
 notempty  app/controllers
 notempty  app
```

script/generate

Generators are used to create instant code for use in a Rails application. When you run the generator (using script/generate), new files (controllers, models, views, etc.) are generated and added to

---

your application. You can also create custom generators. For more information on custom generators, watch Ryan Bates's Railscast at *http://railscasts.com/episodes/58*.

To get more help on the generator script, type:

```
./script/generate --help
```

For help on a specific generator, type:

```
./script/generate [generator] --help
```

Rails comes with several built-in generators.

controller

Stubs out a new controller and its views. Pass the controller name, either CamelCased or under_scored, and a list of views as arguments.

To create a controller within a module, specify the controller name as a path, like *parent_module/controller_name*.

You can also create subcontrollers, which will inherit the parent controller by specifying the controller name as `ParentController-Name::ChildControllerName`. For example, if I have a controller named *admin* and I want a subcontroller named *users* that will inherit the authentication filter in the `AdminController`, I would type:

```
./script/generate controller Admin::Users
```

This generates a controller class in *app/controllers/admin*, view templates in *app/views/admin/controller_name*, a helper class in *app/helpers/admin*, and a functional test suite in *test/functional/admin*.

However, to make the child controller `UsersController` inherit `AdminController`, you will need to add the correct inheritance in *app/controllers/admin/users_controller.rb*:

```
class UsersController < AdminController
```

Usage

```
./script/generate controller ControllerName [options]
```

Example

```
./script/generate controller Product name:string price:decimal
  quantity:integer
```

integration_test

Stubs out a new integration test. Pass the name of the test, either CamelCased or under_scored, as an argument. The new test class is generated in *test/integration/testname_test.rb*.

Usage

```
./script/generate integration_test IntegrationTestName [options]
```

Example

```
./script/generate integration_test GeneralStories
```

mailer

Stubs out a new mailer and its views. Pass the mailer name, either CamelCased or under_scored, and an optional list of emails as arguments.

This generates a mailer class in *app/models*, view templates in *app/views/mailer_name*, a unit test in *test/unit*, and fixtures in *test/fixtures*.

Usage

```
./script/generate mailer MailerName [options]
```

Example

```
./script/generate mailer Notifications signup forgot_password invoice
```

migration

Stubs out a new database migration. Pass the migration name, either CamelCased or under_scored, and an optional list of attribute pairs as arguments.

A migration class is generated in *db/migrate*, prefixed by a timestamp.

You can name your migration whatever you like; however, the preferred standard is to be very descriptive as to the purpose of the script, like *AddColumnsToTable* or *RemoveColumnsFromTable*.

Usage

```
./script/generate migration MigrationName [options]
```

Example

```
./script/generate migration AddLastLoginToUsers last_login:datetime
```

model

Stubs out a new model by generating a new class in *app/models*, a new migration class in *db/migrate*, a unit test in *test/unit*, and a fixture in *test/fixtures*. Pass the model name, either CamelCased or under_scored, and an optional list of attribute pairs as arguments.

Usage

```
./script/generate model ModelName [field:type, field:type]
```

Example

```
./script/generate model Book title:string description:text pages:integer
```

observer

Stubs out a new observer. An observer provides a way to monitor life cycle events of a model object outside of the model itself and lets you avoid cluttering the model class with logic that's not core to the model. For more on observers, visit *http://api.rubyonrails.org/classes/ActiveRecord/Observer.html*.

To generate an observer, pass the observer name, either Camel-Cased or under_scored, as an argument.

The generator creates an observer class in *app/models* and a unit test in *test/unit*.

Usage

```
./script/generate observer ObserverName [options]
```

Example

```
./script/generate observer Account
```

plugin

Stubs out a new plugin. Pass the plugin name, either CamelCased or under_scored, as an argument. Pass --with-generator to add an example generator also.

This creates a plugin in *vendor/plugins* including an *init.rb* and *README*, as well as standard *lib*, *task*, and *test* directories.

Usage

```
./script/generate plugin PluginName [options]
```

Example

```
./script/generate plugin SimpleLayout
```

resource

Stubs out a new resource, including an empty model and controller suitable for a RESTful, resource-oriented application. Pass the singular model name, either CamelCased or under_scored, as the first argument and an optional list of attribute pairs.

Usage

```
./script/generate resource ModelName [field:type, field:type]
```

Example

```
./script/generate resource Post title:string body:text published:boolean
```

scaffold

Scaffolds an entire resource, from model and migration to controller and views, along with a full test suite, and adds the resource to the *config/routes.rb* file. The resource is ready to use as a starting point for your RESTful, resource-oriented application.

Usage

```
./script/generate scaffold ModelName [field:type, field:type]
```

Example

```
./script/generate scaffold Comment user_id:integer body:text
```

session_migration

Creates a migration to add the sessions table used by the ActiveRecord session store. Pass the migration name, either CamelCased or under_scored, as an argument.

Usage

```
./script/generate session_migration SessionMigrationName [options]
```

Example

```
./script/generate session_migration CreateSessionTable
```

For more information on different session types, refer to the "Sessions" section later in this book.

---

script/performance

Rails comes with several scripts to help enhance the performance of the application.

benchmarker

Benchmarks one or more statements a number of times from within the Rails environment.

Usage

```
./script/performance/benchmarker [times] [script] [script] [script] ...
```

Example

```
./script/performance/benchmarker [times] 'Person.do_this' 'Person.do_that'
```

profiler

Profiles a single statement from within the environment.

Usage

```
./script/performance/profiler [script] [times] [flat|graph|graph_html]
```

Example

```
./script/performance/profiler 'Person.do_this(10)' 25 graph
```

request

Wrapper script around the ruby-prof (*http://ruby-prof.rubyforge .org*) library. This script lets you run multiple requests against a URL in your application and get a detailed code profile report in text and HTML.

Usage

```
./script/performance/request [options] [script path]
```

Options

```
-n, --times [0000]
```
How many requests to process (defaults to 100)

```
-b, --benchmark
```
Benchmark instead of profiling

```
--open [CMD]
```
Command to open profile results (defaults to "open %s &")

Example

```
# Create a file called 'perfscript' containing
post('/sessions', { :login => 'berry', :password => 'test' })

# Results
Thread ID: 218880
Total: 21.639647
```

%self	total	self	wait	child	calls	name
19.28	14.08	4.17	0.00	9.91	25200	Pathname#cleanpath_aggressive
17.11	5.36	3.70	0.00	1.66	157800	Pathname#chop_basename
5.38	2.22	1.16	0.00	1.05	50400	Pathname#initialize
4.66	1.50	1.01	0.00	0.49	265600	Kernel#===
3.21	0.69	0.69	0.00	0.00	183000	Regexp#to_s
3.20	0.72	0.69	0.00	0.03	377100	String#==
3.18	1.01	0.69	0.00	0.32	800	Array#select

script/plugin

Rails plugin manager.

Usage

`./script/plugin [OPTIONS] command`

Commands

discover
Discovers plugin repositories

list
Lists available plugins

install
Installs plugin(s) from known repositories or URLs

update
Updates installed plugins

remove
Uninstalls plugins

source
Adds a plugin source repository

unsource
> Removes a plugin repository

sources
> Lists currently configured plugin repositories

script/process

These scripts inspect and assist in controlling the processes.

inspector

Displays system information about Rails dispatchers (or other processes that use *pid* files) through the ps command.

Usage
```
./script/process/inspector [options]
```

Options

-s, --ps=command
> Default:
> *ps -o pid,state,user,start,time,pcpu,vsz,majflt,command*
> *-p %s*

-p, --pidpath=path
> Default: */Users/berry/Sites/clearplay/tmp/pids*

-r, --pattern=pattern
> Default: *dispatch.*.pid*

Example
```
# custom ps, %s is where the pid is interleaved
inspector -s 'ps -o user,start,majflt,pcpu,vsz -p %s'
```

reaper

The reaper is used to restart, reload, gracefully exit, and forcefully exit processes running a Rails dispatcher (or any other process responding to the same signals). This is commonly done when a new version of the application is available, so the existing processes can be updated to use the latest code.

The reaper uses *pid* files to work on the processes and, by default, assumes they are located in *RAILS_ROOT/tmp/pids*.

The reaper actions are:

restart
> Restarts the application by reloading both application and framework codes

reload
> Only reloads the application but not the framework (like the development environment)

graceful
> Marks all of the processes for exit after the next request

kill
> Forcefully exits all processes, regardless of whether they're currently serving a request

Usage

```
./script/process/reaper [options]
```

Options

```
-a, --action=name
    reload|graceful|kill (default: restart)

-p, --pidpath=path
    Default: [RAILS_ROOT]/tmp/pids

-r, --pattern=pattern
    Default: dispatch.[0-9]*.pid
```

Example

```
# kill all processes that keep pids in tmp/pids
reaper -a kill -r *.pid
```

spawner

The spawner is a wrapper for spawn-fcgi and Mongrel that makes it easier to start multiple processes running the Rails dispatcher. The spawn-fcgi command is included with the lighttpd web server but can be used with both Apache and lighttpd (and any other web server supporting externally managed FCGI processes). Mongrel automatically ships with mongrel_rails for starting dispatchers.

Usage

```
./script/process/spawner [platform] [options]
```

Options

-a, --address=ip
  Binds to IP address (default: 0.0.0.0)

-p, --port=number
  Starting port number (default: 8000)

-i, --instances=number
  Number of instances (default: 3)

-r, --repeat=seconds
  Repeats spawn attempts every *n* seconds (default: off)

-e, --environment=name
  Test|development|production (default: production)

-P, --prefix=path
  URL prefix for Rails app (used only with Mongrel v0.3.15 and higher)

-n, --process=name
  Default: dispatch

-s, --spawner=path
  Default: */usr/bin/env spawn-fcgi* (based on OS X install)

-d, --dispatcher=path
  Default: *[RAILS_ROOT]/public/dispatch.fcgi*

Example

```
# starts 10 instances counting from 9100 to 9109 using Mongrel
if available.
./script/process/spawner -p 9100 -i 10
```

script/runner

Runs Ruby code or a specified Ruby file.

Usage

```
./script/runner [options] ('Some.ruby(code)' or a filename)
```

Options

`-e, --environment=name`
> Specifies the environment for the runner to operate under (test, development, or production)

Example

`./script/runner MovieList.update_from_imdb -e production`

TIP

You can also use runner to run Ruby code within shell scripts:

```
#!/usr/bin/env /Users/berry/Sites/myapp/script/runner

Product.find(:all).each { |p| p.price *= 2 ; p.save! }
```

---

script/server

Starts the web server. If you have Mongrel installed, it will run it by default. To force *webrick*, pass webrick as an option.

Usage

`./script/server [options]`

Options

`-p, --port=port`
> Runs Rails on the specified port (default: 3000)

`-b, --binding=ip`
> Binds Rails to the specified IP address (default: 0.0.0.0)

`-d, --daemon`
> Makes server run as a daemon

`-u, --debugger`
> Enables ruby-debugging for the server

`-e, --environment=name`
> Specifies the environment to run this server under (test, development, or production) (default: development)

Environments

Rails environments reflect the stages of development for a typical application: development, test, and production.

You can set the Rails environment by doing one or both of the following:

- Set the `RAILS_ENV` environment variable to the environment name (development, test, or production).
- Modify *config/environment.rb* and update the line (be sure that it is not commented out):

  ```
  ENV['RAILS_ENV'] ||= 'production'
  ```

Within the Rails application, the environment name can be accessed with:

```
RAILS_ENV
```

The three default Rails environments are:

Development

    The development environment is used primarily when developing Rails applications. The application's code is reloaded on every request, which slows down the response time but is ideal, as the developer does not have to restart the server when changes are made.

Test

    The test environment is used exclusively to run your application's test suite. You should never need to work with it otherwise. Remember that your test database is scratch space for the test suite and is wiped and recreated between test runs. *Don't rely on the data there!*

Production

    The production environment is meant for finished, "live" apps. Code is not reloaded between requests, but the response time is much faster than that of the development mode.

Configuring Your Environment

Three environment files—*development.rb*, *test.rb*, and *production.rb*—are generated in the *config/environments* folder when the Rails application is created. Each contains configuration settings for their respective environments.

Although there are default configuration settings, any of the options can be changed.

General options

Each of these options should be prepended with `config.` when used with a `Rails::Initializer do |config|` block:

`cache_classes`
> Whether or not classes should be cached (set to `false` if you want application classes to be reloaded on each request).

`controller_paths`
> The list of paths that should be searched for controllers (defaults to *app/controllers* and *components*).

`database_configuration_file`
> The path to the database configuration file to use (defaults to *config/database.yml*).

`frameworks`
> The list of Rails framework components that should be loaded (defaults to `:active_record`, `:action_control ler`, `:action_view`, `:action_mailer`, and `:action_web_service`).

`load_paths`
> An array option of additional paths to prepend to the load path. By default, all *app*, *lib*, *vendor*, and *mock* paths are included in this list.

`log_level`
> The log level to use for the default Rails logger. In production mode, this defaults to `:info`. In development mode, it defaults to `:debug`.

log_path

The path to the logfile to use. Defaults to *log/#{environ ment}.log* (e.g., *log/development.log* or *log/production.log*).

logger

The specific logger to use. By default, a logger will be created and initialized using **log_path** and **log_level**, but a programmer may specifically set the logger to use via this accessor, and it will be used directly.

view_path

The root of the application's views. Defaults to *app/views*.

whiny_nils

Set to **true** if you want to be warned when you try to invoke any method of **nil**. Set to **false** for the standard Ruby behavior.

plugins

The list of plugins to load. If this is set to **nil**, all plugins will be loaded. If this is set to [ ], no plugins will be loaded. Otherwise, plugins will be loaded in the order specified.

plugin_paths

The path to the root of the plugins directory. By default, it is in *vendor/plugins*.

plugin locators

The classes that handle finding the desired plugins that you'd like to load for your application. By default, it is the **Rails::Plugin::FileSystemLocator**, which finds plugins to load in *vendor/plugins* You can hook into gem location by subclassing **Rails::Plugin::Locator** and adding it onto the list of **plugin_locators**.

plugin_loader

The class that handles loading each plugin. Defaults to **Rails::Plugin::Loader**, but a subclass would have access to fine-grained modification of the loading behavior. See the implementation of **Rails::Plugin::Loader** for more details.

ActiveRecord options

When used with a `Rails::Initializer do |config|` block, each of these options should be prepended with `config.active_record.`:

primary_key_prefix_type
> Accessor for the prefix type that will be prepended to every primary key column name. The options are `:table_name` and `:table_name_with_underscore`. If the first is specified, the `Product` class will look for *productid* instead of *id* as the primary column. If the latter is specified, the `Product` class will look for *product_id* instead of *id*. Remember that this is a global setting for all ActiveRecords.

table_name_prefix
> The string to prepend to every table name. By default, the prefix is an empty string.

table_name_suffix
> The same as `table_name_prefix`, but it appends the string to the table name.

pluralize_table_names
> Indicates whether or not table names should be the pluralized versions of the corresponding class names (defaults to `true`).

colorize_logging
> Should logs have ANSI color codes in logging statments? (Defaults to `true`.)

default_timezone
> Determines whether to use `Time.local` (using `:local`) or `Time.utc` (using `:utc`) when pulling dates and times from the database (defaults to `:local`).

allow_concurrency
> Determines whether to use a connection for each thread or a single shared connection for all threads (defaults to `false`). Set to `true` if you're writing a threaded application.

`schema_format`
> Specifies whether to dump the database in *ruby* or *sql*. It takes `:ruby` or `:sql` as options, and defaults to `:ruby`.

ActionView options

Each of the following options should be prepended with `config.action_view.` when used with a `Rails::Initializer do |config|` block:

`erb_trim_mode`
> Specifies trim mode for the ERB compiler (defaults to "-").

`cache_template_loading`
> Specifies whether file extension lookup should be cached and whether template base path lookup should be cached. Should be `false` for development environments (defaults to `true`).

`debug_rjs`
> Specifies whether RJS responses should be wrapped in a try/catch block that alerts the caught exception (and then re-raises it).

ActionMailer options

Each of the following options should be prepended with `config.action_mailer.` when used with a `Rails::Initializer do |config|` block:

`template_root`
> Template root determines the base from which template references will be made.

`logger`
> The logger is used for generating information on the mailing run, if available. Can be set to `nil` for no logging. Compatible with both Ruby's own Logger and Log4r loggers.

`smtp_settings`
> Allows detailed configuration for *:smtp* delivery method:

:address

Allows you to use a remote mail server. Just change it from its default `localhost` setting.

:port

On the off chance that your mail server doesn't run on port 25, you can change it.

:domain

If you need to specify a HELO domain, you can do it here.

:user_name

If your mail server requires authentication, set the username in this setting.

:password

If your mail server requires authentication, set the password in this setting.

:authentication

If your mail server requires authentication, you need to specify the authentication type here. The available options are `:plain`, `:login`, and `:cram_md5`.

sendmail_settings

Allows you to override options for the `:sendmail` delivery method:

:location

The location of the sendmail executable (defaults to */usr/sbin/sendmail*)

:arguments

The command-line arguments

raise_delivery_errors

Whether or not errors should be raised if the email fails to be delivered. Defaults to `true`.

delivery_method

Defines a delivery method. Possible values are `:smtp` (default), `:sendmail`, and `:test`.

---

perform_deliveries
> Determines whether deliver_* methods are actually carried out. By default, they are, but this can be turned off to help functional testing.

deliveries
> Keeps an array of all the emails sent out through the ActionMailer with delivery_method :test. Most useful for unit and functional testing.

default_charset
> The default charset used for the body and to encode the subject (defaults to utf-8). You can also pick a different charset from inside a method with @charset.

default_content_type
> The default content type used for the main part of the message (defaults to text/plain). You can also use @content_type to pick a different content type from inside a method.

default_mime_version
> The default mime version used for the message. Defaults to 1.0. You can also pick a different value from inside a method with @mime_version.

default_implicit_parts_order
> When a message is built implicitly (i.e., multiple parts are assembled from templates that specify the content type in their filenames), this variable controls how the parts are ordered. Defaults to ["text/html", "text/enriched", "text/plain"]. Items that appear first in the array have higher priority in the mail client and appear last in the mime-encoded message. You can also pick a different order from inside a method with @implicit_parts_order.

Custom Environments

Rails applications are not constrained to the development, test, and production environments. You can create any number of additional Rails environment configurations very easily.

Let's assume the company you are working for has a staging server for internal testing, and it is a mirror of the live production server. There may be some things that you would prefer to not act as live on the staging server, so an additional environment may be just the thing.

To create a new environment called staging, do the following:

1. Create the file *config/environments/staging.rb*. This will contain all of the configurations that are specific to this environment. You can copy these from the other enviroment files and modify as desired.

2. Add staging to the *config/database.yml* file with the appropriate database settings and name.

3. Create the database and run the migrate scripts (see the upcoming section "Migrations").

Now you can run your Rails application with the new environment.

Rake

Rake is a build tool that helps you build, compile, or otherwise process files, sometimes in large numbers. It's similar to Make (*http://www.gnu.org/software/make*) and Apache Ant (*http://ant.apache.org/*), but it is written in Ruby. Ruby uses it in many applications, not just Rails, but Rails operations use Rake frequently.

Rake uses a Rakefile to figure out what to do. A Rakefile contains named tasks. When you create a Rails project, a Rakefile is automatically created to help you deal with a variety of jobs, such as running tests, looking at project statistics, and migrating database schemas.

Rake was written by Jim Weirich (*http://onestepback.org/*). Go to *http://rake.rubyforge.org/* to find documentation on Rake. Also, a good introduction to Rake, by Martin Fowler, can be found at *http://www.martinfowler.com/articles/rake.html*.

To see whether Rake is present on your computer, type:

```
rake --version
```

An affirmative response would look similar to this:

```
rake, version 0.8.1
```

If this command fails, use RubyGems to install Rake:

```
sudo gem install rake
```

To get help on Rake, type:

```
rake --help
```

To view the list of Rake tasks available, type:

```
rake --tasks
```

To see project statistics for a Rails application, in the application root folder, type:

```
rake stats
```

To use the most recent development version of Rails, known as EdgeRails, type:

```
rake rails:freeze:edge
```

Alternatively, you can freeze any previous version of Rails:

```
rake rails:freeze:edge TAG=rel_2-0-2
```

To unfreeze Rails and use the default system install, you can type:

```
rake rails:unfreeze
```

Usage and Options

Usage

```
rake [-f rakefile] {options} targets...
```

Options

```
-C, --classic-namespace
```
Puts Task and FileTask in the top level namespace

```
-D, --describe
```
Describes the tasks (matching optional PATTERN), then exits

-n, --dry-run
Does a dry run without executing actions

-h, --help
Displays this list of options

-I, --libdir=LIBDIR
Includes LIBDIR in the search path for required modules

-N, --nosearch
Does not search parent directories for the Rakefile

-P, --prereqs
Displays the tasks and dependencies, then exits

-q, --quiet
Does not log messages to standard output

-f, --rakefile
Uses FILE as the Rakefile

-R, --rakelibdir=RAKELIBDIR
Auto-imports any *.rake* files in *RAKELIBDIR* (default is *rakelib*)

-r, --require=MODULE
Requires MODULE before executing Rakefile

-s, --silent
Like --quiet, also suppresses the *in directory* announcement

-T, --tasks
Displays the tasks (matching optional PATTERN) with descriptions, then exits

-t, --trace
Turns on invoke/execute tracing and enables full backtrace

-v, --verbose
Logs message to standard output (default)

-V, --version
Displays the installed version of Rake

Building Custom Rake Tasks

At times, you may want to create custom Rake tasks to perform actions that the default tasks do not.

As an example, let's create a Rake task that will find users whose subscriptions are about to expire and send them an email:

1. Create a new Rakefile in the *lib/tasks* folder called *utils.rake*.

2. Add the following Rake tasks into *utils.rake*:

```
namespace :utils do
  desc "Finds soon to expire subscriptions
  and emails users"
  task(:send_expire_soon_emails => :environment) do
    # Find users to email
    for user in User.members_soon_to_expire
      puts "Emailing #{user.name}"
      UserNotifier.deliver_expire_soon_notification(user)
    end
  end
end
```

(Note that by using `=> :environment`, you have access to your models.)

3. Now to run the script, type the following in the command line:

```
rake utils:send_expire_soon_emails

# or to run this in production mode
rake RAILS_ENV=production utils:send_expire_soon_emails
```

4. This task can also be added to your cronjob:

```
0 0 * * * cd /var/www/apps/rails_app/ && /usr/local/bin/rake \
          RAILS_ENV=production utils:send_expire_soon_emails
```

For additional resources on custom Rake tasks, there is a great tutorial at *http://www.railsenvy.com/2007/6/11/ruby-on-rails-rake-tutorial*. You can also find a Railscast by Ryan Bates at *http://railscasts.com/episodes/66*.

Testing Rails

Testing has become vital to building high-quality software that is to stand the test of time. With proper testing, you can minimize rewriting code and avoid spending time debugging it. This documentation is adapted and abbreviated from the Ruby on Rails online manual, chapters 21–28 (*http://manuals.ru byonrails.com/read/chapter/21*).

NOTE

According to a poll done on RailsEnvy.com, about 61% of Rails developers use RSpec (*http://rspec.info*), whereas only about 24% prefer the built-in Test Unit framework that is shipped with Rails. RSpec is definitely worth looking into, as are other methods of testing that I don't cover in this book such as test-driven development (*http://www.testdriven.com*) and Selenium IDE for Firefox (*http://selenium.openqa.org*).

In Rails, these three types of tests have very specific meanings that may differ from what you expect:

Functional tests
Used for testing controllers

Unit tests
Used for testing models

Integration tests
Used for testing higher-level scenarios that exercise interactions between controllers

Assertions

An assertion is a single line of code that evaluates an expression and tests the results against an expected value. For example, you might assert that a password is at least six characters long; failing an assertion fails the associated test.

Rails currently has six categories of assertions.

DOM assertions

`assert_dom_equal(expected, actual, message = "")`
Tests two HTML strings for equivalency (e.g., identical up to re-ordering of attributes).

`assert_dom_not_equal(expected, actual, message = "")`
The negated form of `assert_dom_equivalent`.

Model assertions

`assert_valid(record)`
Ensures that the passed record is valid by ActiveRecord standards and returns any error messages if it is not.

Response assertions

`assert_redirected_to(options = {}, message=nil)`
Asserts that the redirection options passed in match those of the redirect called in the latest action. This match can be partial, such that `assert_redirected_to(:controller => "weblog")` will also match the redirection of `redirect_to(:controller => "weblog", :action => "show")`, and so on.

`assert_response(type, message = nil)`
Asserts that the response is one of the following types:

> `:success`
> Status code is 200.

> `:redirect`
> Status code is in the 300–399 range.

> `:missing`
> Status code is 404.

> `:error`
> Status code is in the 500–599 range.

You can also pass an explicit status number, such as assert_response(501) or its symbolic equivalent, assert_response(:not_implemented).

assert_template(expected = nil, message=nil)

Asserts that the request was rendered with the appropriate template file.

Routing assertions

assert_generates(expected_path, options, defaults={}, extras = {}, message=nil)

Asserts that the provided options can be used to generate the provided path. This is the inverse of assert_recognizes. The extras parameter is used to tell the request the names and values of additional request parameters that would be in a query string. The message parameter allows you to specify a custom error message for assertion failures.

The defaults parameter is unused.

assert_recognizes(expected_options, path, extras={}, message=nil)

Asserts that the routing of the given path was handled correctly and that the parsed options (given in the expected_options hash) match path. Basically, it asserts that Rails recognizes the route given by expected_options.

Pass a hash in the second argument (path) to specify the request method. This is useful for routes requiring a specific HTTP method. The hash should contain a :path with the incoming request path and a :method containing the required HTTP verb:

```
# assert that POSTing to /items will call the create action
on ItemsController
assert_recognizes({:controller => 'items', :action
                    => 'create'},
                  {:path => 'items', :method => :post})
```

You can also pass in extras with a hash containing URL parameters that would normally be in the query string. This can be used to assert that values in the query string will end up in the params hash correctly. To test query strings, you must use the extras argument; appending the query string on the path directly will not work.

Example:

```
# assert that a path of '/items/list/1?view=print'
# returns the correct options
assert_recognizes(
    {
      :controller => 'items',
      :action => 'list', :id => '1',
      :view => 'print'
    },
    'items/list/1', { :view => "print" })
```

The message parameter allows you to pass in an error message that is displayed upon failure.

`assert_routing(path,    options,    defaults={},    extras={}, message=nil)`

>   Asserts that `path` and `options` match both ways; in other words, it verifies that `path` generates `options` and then that `options` generates `path`. This essentially combines `assert_recognizes` and `assert_generates` into one step.

>   The `extras` hash allows you to specify options that would normally be provided as a query string to the action. The `message` parameter allows you to specify a custom error message to display upon failure.

Selector assertions

`assert_select(element, selector, equality?, message?)`

>   An assertion that selects elements and makes one or more equality tests.

>   If the first argument is an element, selects all matching elements starting from (and including) that element and all its children in depth-first order.

>   If no element is specified, calling `assert_select` will select from the response HTML. Calling `assert_select` inside an `assert_select` block will run the assertion for each element selected by the enclosing assertion.

Example:

```
assert_select "ol>li" do |elements|
  elements.each do |element|
    assert_select element, "li"
  end
end
```

Or for short:

```
assert_select "ol>li" do
  assert_select "li"
end
```

`assert_select_email { }`

> Extracts the body of an email and runs nested assertions on it.
>
> You must enable deliveries for this assertion to work. Use:
>
> ```
> ActionMailer::Base.perform_deliveries = true
> ```

`assert_select_encoded(element?) { |elements| ... }`

> Extracts the content of an element, treats it as encoded HTML, and runs nested assertions on it.
>
> You typically call this method within another assertion to operate on all currently selected elements. You can also pass an element or array of elements.
>
> The content of each element is unencoded and wrapped in the root element `encoded`. It then calls the block with all unencoded elements.

`assert_select_rjs(*args) { |matches| ... }`

> Selects content from the RJS response.

Narrowing down.

With no arguments, asserts that one or more elements are updated or inserted by RJS statements.

Use the `id` argument to narrow down the assertion to only statements that update or insert an element with that identifier.

Use the first argument to narrow down assertions to only statements of that type. Possible values are `:replace`, `:replace_html`, `:show`, `:hide`, `:toggle`, `:remove`, and `:insert_html`.

Use the argument `:insert` followed by an insertion position to narrow down the assertion to only statements that insert elements in that position. Possible values are `:top`, `:bottom`, `:before`, and `:after`.

Using the :remove statement, you will be able to pass a block, but it will be ignored as there is no HTML passed for this statement.

Using blocks.

Without a block, assert_select_rjs merely asserts that the response contains one or more RJS statements that replace or update content.

With a block, assert_select_rjs also selects all elements used in these statements and passes them to the block. Nested assertions are supported.

Calling assert_select_rjs with no arguments and using nested asserts will assert that the HTML content is returned by one or more RJS statements. Using assert_select directly makes the same assertion on the content but without distinguishing whether the content is returned in an HTML or JavaScript.

css_select(*args)
> Select and return all matching elements.
>
> If called with a single argument, uses that argument as a selector to match all elements of the current page. Returns an empty array if no match is found.
>
> If called with two arguments, uses the first argument as the base element and the second argument as the selector. Attempts to match the base element and any of its children. Returns an empty array if no match is found.

Tag assertions

assert_no_tag(*opts)
> Identical to assert_tag but asserts that a matching tag does not exist. (See assert_tag for a full discussion of the syntax.)

assert_tag(*opts)
> Asserts that there is a tag/node/element in the body of the response that meets all of the given conditions. The conditions parameter must be a hash of any of the following keys (all are optional):
>
> :tag
>> The node type must match the corresponding value.

:attributes

A hash. The node's attributes must match the corresponding values in the hash.

:parent

A hash. The node's parent must match the corresponding hash.

:child

A hash. At least one of the node's immediate children must meet the criteria described by the hash.

:ancestor

A hash. At least one of the node's ancestors must meet the criteria described by the hash.

:descendant

A hash. At least one of the node's descendants must meet the criteria described by the hash.

:sibling

A hash. At least one of the node's siblings must meet the criteria described by the hash.

:after

A hash. The node must be after any sibling meeting the criteria described by the hash, and at least one sibling must match.

:before

A hash. The node must be before any sibling meeting the criteria described by the hash, and at least one sibling must match.

:children

A hash, for counting children of a node. Accepts these keys:

:count

Either a number or a range that must equal (or include) the number of children that match.

:less_than

The number of matching children must be less than this number.

:greater_than
> The number of matching children must be greater than this number.

:only
> Another hash consisting of the keys to use to match the children; only matching children will be counted.

:content
> The textual content of the node must match the given value. This will not match HTML tags in the body of a tag—only text.

Conditions are matched using the following algorithms:

- If the condition is a string, it must be a substring of the value.
- If the condition is a regexp, it must match the value.
- If the condition is a number, the value must match number.to_s.
- If the condition is true, the value must not be nil.
- If the condition is false or nil, the value must be nil.

Functional Tests

In Rails, you'll use functional tests to exercise one feature, or function, in your controllers. Functional and integration tests check the responses to web commands, called *HTTP requests*.

Some questions that functional tests might address are.

- Was the web request successful?
- Were we redirected to the right page?
- Were we successfully authenticated?
- Was the correct object stored in the response template?

Just as there is a one-to-one ratio between unit tests and models, so is there between functional tests and controllers. For a controller named HomeController, you would have a test case named HomeControllerTest.

Here is an example of a functional test:

```ruby
require File.dirname(__FILE__) + '/../test_helper'

# grab our UsersController because we're going to test it
require 'users_controller'

# Raise errors beyond the default web-based presentation
class UsersController; def rescue_action(e) raise e end; end

class UsersControllerTest < Test::Unit::TestCase
  def setup
    @controller = UsersController.new
    @request = ActionController::TestRequest.new
    @response = ActionController::TestResponse.new
  end

  # let's test our main index page
  def test_index
    get :index
    assert_response :success
  end
end
```

In the setup method, we create three objects:

- One of your controllers to be tested (`@controller`)
- A TestRequest to simulate a web request (`@request`)
- A TestResponse to provide information about the test request (`@response`)

Ninety-nine percent, if not one hundred percent, of your functional tests will have these three objects in the setup.

In the `test_index` method, we use the objects created from the setup method and then the `get` protocol to get the response from the `:index` action. We then assert that the response type was a `:success`.

All of the request types are methods that you can use; however, you'll probably end up using the first two more often than the others. There are five request types supported in Rails:

- get
- post
- put
- head

- delete

Controller-driven functional tests

Here are two test cases that are used to test authentication:

```
def test_failing_authenticate
  process 'authenticate', { "user_name" => "missing_password",
  "password"  => "" }
  assert_redirect_url "http://localhost:3000/login/"
end

def test_succesful_authentication
  process 'authenticate', { "user_name" => "cavneb", "password"  =>
  "mysecret" }
  assert_redirect_url "http://localhost:3000/dashboard/"
end
```

The **process** method fires up the controller with a given action
(the first parameter), as well as optional request parameters
(e.g., **form post** variables).

Then, once the response has been generated, you can inter-
rogate it and see if all went well.

View-driven functional tests

It's a good idea to require that the views emit well-formed, valid
XHTML. This allows you to analyze the results with an XML
parser:

```
def test_show_conversation
  ...
  response = ForumController.process_test(@request)
  ...
  # parse the resulting HIML into a REXML..Document object
  # if the output is not a well-formed XML, an exception is thrown
  output = Document.new(response.body)
  # and here you can use REXML APIs, including XPath
  # to retrieve pieces of data from the XML

end
```

Here is one example of how **REXML::XPath** can be used to test
template output:

```
...
require 'rexml/document'
...
  def test_show
```

```
@request.path    = '/test/show'
@request.action = 'show'
@request.request_parameters['id'] = '1'

response = ConversationController.process_test(@request)

# Parse the response body
xml = nil
assert_nothing_thrown { xml = REXML::Document.new(response.body) }

# Retrieve all hyperlinks from somewhere deep inside the response
title_hrefs = REXML::XPath.match(xml,
    '/html/body/table/tr[2]/td/table/tr[1]/td/a')

# Check that there are three hyperlinks...
assert_equal 3, title_hrefs.size

# ... and they point where they should
href_urls = title_hrefs.map {|element|
  element.attribute('href').value }.sort
assert_equal ['/conversation/show?id=1', '/forum/?id=1',
    '/message/new?conv_id=1'], href_urls
end
```

For more information on functional testing, visit *http://wiki.ru byonrails.org/rails/pages/HowtoFunctionalTest*.

Fixtures

Fixtures allow you to populate your testing database with pre-defined data before your tests run. They are database-independent and assume one of two formats: YAML or comma-separated value (CSV).

You'll find fixtures under your *test/fixtures* directory. When you run `script/generate model` to create a new model, fixture stubs will be automatically created and placed in this directory.

YAML

YAML is a human-friendly data serialization standard for all programming languages:

```
# Example YAML File

eric:
  id: 1
  name: Eric Berry
  birthday: 1977-04-15
```

```
    profession: Software Engineer

aubree:
  id: 2
  name: Aubree Berry
  birthday: 1985-11-30
  profession: Medical Assistant
```

Each fixture is given a **name** followed by an indented list of colon-separated key/value pairs. Records are separated by a blank space. You can place comments by using the # character in the first column.

Comma-separated value

Fixtures can also be described using the all too familiar comma-separated value file format. These files, just like YAML fixtures, are placed in the *test/fixtures* directory, but they end with the *.csv* file extension (as in *test_users.csv*).

A CSV fixture looks like this:

```
id, name, birthday, profession
1, "Eric Berry", 1977-04-15, "Software Engineer"
2, "Aubree Berry", 1985-11-30, "Medical Assistant"
```

The first line is the header; it is a comma-separated list of fields. The rest of the file contains the record data. A few notes about this format:

*   Each cell is stripped of outward-facing spaces.
*   If you use a comma as data, the cell must be encased in quotes.
*   If you use a quote as data, you must escape it with a second quote.
*   Don't use blank lines.
*   Nulls can be achieved just by placing a comma.

Unlike the YAML format, where you give each fixture a name, CSV fixture names are automatically generated. They follow a pattern of model-name-counter. In the previous example, you would have:

```
test-users-1
test-users-2
```

The CSV format is great to use if you have existing data in a spreadsheet or database and are able to save it (or export it) as a CSV.

ERb in YAML and CSV

ERb allows you to embed Ruby code within templates. Both the YAML and CSV fixture formats are preprocessed with ERb, which allows you to use Ruby to help you generate some sample data:

```
<% average_weight = 100 -%>

average:
  id: 1
  weight: <%= average_weight %>

heavy:
  id: 2
  weight: <%= average_weight * 2 %>

light:
  id: 3
  weight: <%= average_weight / 2 %>
```

Mocks

Mocks are classes that load last in your test environment and are intended to override class methods that should not be performed. For example, if part of your test includes interaction with external web services, such as a payment gateway, you may not want the test to pass data to the web service.

This might be our class and method that is sending data to the payment gateway:

```
class PaymentGateway
  ...

  def process_order
    # Code that commits order to payment processor
```

To create a mock, you simply write a class in the *test/mocks/ [environment]* folder:

```
require 'path/to/payment_gateway'

class PaymentGateway
  def process_order  # Method overrides actual PaymentGateway
    process_order
    true
  end
end
```

Unit Testing for Models

In Rails, unit tests are for testing your models. Let's assume that we are testing the Product model, which has the following validations in place:

```
# app/models/Product.rb

class < ActiveRecord::Base
  validates_presence_of     :name, :price, :quantity
  validates_numericality_of :quantity
  validates_uniqueness_of   :name
  validate                  :price_must_be_greater_than_zero

  protected
    def price_must_be_greater_than_zero
      errors.add(:price, 'should be at least 0.01') if price.nil?
      || price < 0.01
    end
end
```

Looking at the validators, you already know what to test for in your unit test. Let's begin by creating the fixtures that we will use:

```
# test/fixtures/products.yml

soccer_ball:
  name:     Soccer Ball
  price:    17.50
  quantity: 25
```

Now that we have the fixtures, let's create the unit tests:

```
# test/unit/product_test.rb

require File.dirname(__FILE__) + '/../test_helper'

class ProductTest < ActiveSupport::TestCase

  # Load fixtures that we created for testing
  fixtures :products
```

```ruby
def test_invalid_with_empty_attributes
  product = Product.new
  assert !product.valid?
end

def test_name_error_with_empty_attributes
  product = Product.new
  product.valid? # Triggers validation
  assert !product.errors.invalid?(:name)
end

def test_price_error_with_empty_attributes
  product = Product.new
  product.valid? # Triggers validation
  assert !product.errors.invalid?(:price)
end

def test_quantity_error_with_empty_attributes
  product = Product.new
  product.valid? # Triggers validation
  assert !product.errors.invalid?(:quantity)
end

def test_invalid_with_duplicate_name
  product = Product.new(:name     => products(:soccer_ball).name,
                        :price    => 20.00,
                        :quantity => 30)
  product.save
  assert_equal "has already been taken", product.errors.on(:name)
end

def test_invalid_with_price_less_than_or_equal_to_zero
  product = Product.new(:name     => 'Tennis Ball',
                        :price    => 0.00,
                        :quantity => 3)
  product.save
  assert_equal "should be at least 0.01", product.errors.on(:price)
end
end
```

Now that the test is created, there are two ways that you can run the test. You can either run it directly with Ruby:

```
ruby test/unit/product_test.rb
```

or you can run all your tests together using the rake command test:

```
rake test
```

After running a test, you should see something like this:

```
Loaded suite test/unit/product_test
Started
```

```
...
Finished in 0.044915 seconds.

3 tests, 8 assertions, 0 failures, 0 errors
```

TIP

It is usually considered best practice to have only one
assert in each test. This way, all your tests get run, and
you save debug time.

Rails Console

The Rails console is a tool that I use almost every time I sit
down to code; it is the secret weapon for Rails developers. The
Rails console is the interactive Ruby shell, or *irb*, in which the
Rails application is loaded. With it you can:

- Debug your code
- View the results of any code snippet
- Perform CRUD on models using ActiveRecord

To start the console from your Rails application root, type:

```
./script/console
```

```
# or you can load a specific environment
./script console production
```

You should see something like the following:

```
Loading development environment (Rails 2.1.0)
>>
```

The >> is the prompt for your Ruby commands.

To exit the console, type **exit** or use Ctrl-z.

Console Tips and Tricks

There are some less well-known features of the Rails console
that may be very useful to you.

Accessing the last return value with _

When using the console, you may sometimes forget to assign a returned value to a variable for additional use. The console provides a magic variable (_) that is assigned the last value your console returned.

Example:

```
>> Movie.first
=> #<Movie id: 1, title: "11th Hour, The", created_at:
"2008-04-10 00:24:06",
updated_at: "2008-04-10 00:24:06">
>> m = _
=> #<Movie id: 1, title: "11th Hour, The", created_at:
"2008-04-10 00:24:06",
updated_at: "2008-04-10 00:24:06">
>> m.title
=> "11th Hour, The"
```

Run the console in sandbox mode

Let's say you needed to test a portion of your code on a live environment but didn't want to make any changes to the database. You can do this with the --sandbox option of the console.

Example:

```
./script/console production --sandbox
Loading production environment in sandbox (Rails 2.1.0)
Any modifications you make will be rolled back on exit
>> movie = Movie.find(:first)
=> #<Movie id: 1, title: "11th Hour, The", created_at:
"2008-04-10 00:24:06",
updated_at: "2008-04-10 00:24:06">
>> movie.title = "Eleventh Hour, The"
=> "Eleventh Hour, The"
>> movie.save
=> true
>> exit

# Now reload the console
./script/console production
Loading production environment (Rails 2.1.0)
>> Movie.find(:first)
=> #<Movie id: 1, title: "11th Hour, The", created_at:
"2008-04-10 00:24:06",
updated_at: "2008-04-10 00:24:06">
```

Output object to YAML with y

When viewing objects in the Rails console, you may find them a bit difficult to read. The y command will make the object easier to read.

Example:

```
>> movie = Movie.find(:first)
=> #<Movie id: 1, title: "11th Hour, The", created_at:
"2008-04-10 00:24:06", updated_at: "2008-04-10 00:24:06">
>> y movie
--- !ruby/object:Movie
attributes:
  updated_at: 2008-04-10 00:24:06
  title: 11th Hour, The
  id: "1"
  created_at: 2008-04-10 00:24:06
attributes_cache: {}

=> nil
>>
```

Format with helper methods using helper

To access the helper methods from within the Rails app console, you can use the object helper.

Examples:

```
>> helper.pluralize(3, 'bottle')
=> "3 bottles"

>> helper.text_area(:foo, :bar)
=> "<textarea cols=\"40\" id=\"foo_bar\" name=\"foo[bar]\"
rows=\"20\"></textarea>"
```

Access your controllers with app

You are able to access your project's controller from within the console using the object app. With this, you are able to make HTTP requests to your controller.

Examples:

```
>> app.class
=> ActionController::Integration::Session

# Get the response from a request to '/movies'
>> app.get '/movies'
=> 200
```

```
# See the contents of the 'flash' hash variable
>> app.flash
=> {}

# View the cookies for this Rails app
>> app.cookies
=> {"_clearplay_session"=>"BAh7BiIKZmxhc2hJQzonQWNOaW9b9d47a75dd0e6"}
```

For more tips on using the Rails console, visit Amy Hoy's blog at *http://slash7.com/articles/2006/12/21/secrets-of-the-rails -console-ninjas* or Ryan Bates's Railscast at *http://railscasts .com/episodes/48*.

ActiveRecord and Models

ActiveRecord connects business objects and database tables to create a persistable domain model where logic and data is presented in one wrapping. For more on ActiveRecord, go to *http: //ar.rubyonrails.com*.

Migrations

Think of migrations as a version repository for the database schema. With migrations, you are able to create versions of your database schema and go forward or backward to whichever version you want. This makes it very convenient for developers who want to just add small changes to a table without having to rebuild the whole database.

Rails provides a generator for creating migrations:

```
./script generate migration MigrationName [options]
```

In the previous example, the generator creates a migration class in *db/migrate* with its version number prefixed to the name. In Rails 2.1, UTC-based migrations were introduced, which use a unique prefix that is less likely to conflict with another migration that somebody else happens to check in around the same time.

Example:

```
class CreateMovies < ActiveRecord::Migration
  def self.up
    create_table :movies do |t|
      t.string  :title
      t.integer :genre_id
      t.string  :rating, :limit => 5
      t.string  :short_description
      t.text    :long_description
      t.boolean :is_new_release, :default => false
      t.timestamps
    end

    # Add foreign key
    add_index :movies, :genre_id
  end

  def self.down
    drop_table :movies
  end
end
```

In this example, we are creating a table named *movies* with the columns *title*, *genre_id*, *rating*, *short_description*, *long_description*, and *is_new_release*. The standard timestamps are also generated, being *created_at* and *updated_at*. The previous example also creates the foreign key indexing.

Column type mappings

Table 1-2 shows a list of generated column types based on the database being used.

Table 1-2. Column mapping chart

Migration type	MySQL	PostgreSQL	SQLite	Oracle
:string	varchar(255)	character varying (255)	varchar(255)	varchar2(255)
:text	text	text	text	clob
:integer	int(11)	integer	integer	number(38)
:float	float	float	float	number
:decimal	decimal	decimal	decimal	decimal
:datetime	datetime	timestamp	datetime	date
:timestamp	datetime	timestamp	datetime	date
:time	time	time	datetime	date

Migration type	MySQL	PostgreSQL	SQLite	Oracle
:date	date	date	date	date
:binary	blob	bytea	blob	blog
:boolean	tinyint(1)	boolean	boolean	number(1)

Column options

Column types also allow options. For example, to create a string column that has only 55 characters in the table, you could use this:

```
t.string :address, :limit => 55
```

Here are the available options and the column types with which they can be used:

`:default => value`
> Sets a default value to the value specified. This can be used by all column types.

`:limit => size`
> Adds a size parameter to string, text, binary, or integer columns.

`:null => true`
> Makes the column required at the database level by setting a *not null* constraint on the column.

`:precision => number`
> Total digits in a number. Only to be used with `:decimal` types.

`:scale => number`
> Total digits to the right of the decimal point. Only to be used with `:decimal` types.

Run the migration

To run the migration script, type:

```
rake db:migrate
```

This will run all of your new migration scripts and update the database.

To run a migration script on a specific environment, you can use:

```
rake db:migrate RAILS_ENV=[environment]
```

Associations

Associations are a class method used for establishing object relations through foreign keys. By using associations, relationships, such as "User has many Comments" or "Comment belongs to a Movie," are established automatically. Each macro adds a number of methods to the class; the methods are specialized according to the collection or association symbol and the options hash. It works much the same way as Ruby's own *attr* methods. For more on associations, go to *http://api.rubyon rails.org/classes/ActiveRecord/Associations/ClassMethods .html*.

The standard associations are as follows.

One-to-one

Use `has_one` in the base and `belongs_to` in the associated model:

```
class Picture < ActiveRecord::Base
  has_one :thumbnail
end
class Thumbnail < ActiveRecord::Base
  belongs_to :picture
end
```

See Figure 1-1.

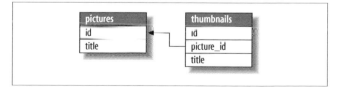

Figure 1-1. One-to-one associations

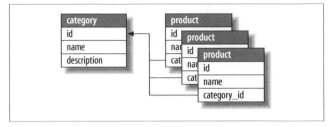

Figure 1-2. One-to-many associations

One-to-many

Use `has_many` in the base and `belongs_to` in the associated model:

```
class Category < ActiveRecord::Base
  has_many :products
end
class Product < ActiveRecord::Base
  belongs_to :category
end
```

See Figure 1-2.

Many-to-many

There are two ways to build a many-to-many relationship. The first and preferred way uses a `has_many` association with the `:through` option and a join model, so there are two stages of associations:

```
class UserRole < ActiveRecord::Base
  belongs_to :user
  belongs_to :role
end

class User < ActiveRecord::Base
  has_many :user_roles
  has_many :roles, :through => :user_roles
end

class Role < ActiveRecord::Base
  has_many :user_roles
  has_many :users, :through => :user_roles
end
```

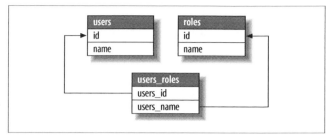

Figure 1-3. Many-to-many associations

The second way uses **has_and_belongs_to_many** in both models. This requires a join table that has no corresponding model or primary key:

```
class User < ActiveRecord::Base
  has_and_belongs_to_many :roles
end

class Role < ActiveRecord::Base
  has_and_belongs_to_many :users
end
```

See Figure 1-3.

Polymorphic associations

Polymorphic associations are models that can be used as one or more model classes.

There are three steps to setting up polymorphic associations:

1. Declare the interface.

    The class that is to be used as the associated model creates an interface that other models can associate with.

    For example, **Address** exposes an interface named addressable:

    ```
    class Address < ActiveRecord::Base
      belongs_to :addressable, :polymorphic => true
    end
    ```

The association **belongs_to** must have a name and the attribute **:polymorphic**.

2. Create an association to the interface.

Any class that will associate with our shared class must declare that association through the *interface* previously declared.

For example, User associates with the Address class through addressable:

```
class User < ActiveRecord::Base
  has_one :address, :as => :addressable
end
```

The association (has_one in this case) has a name and refers to the interface via the :as attribute. Possible associations are has_one and has_many.

3. Use the association the way you normally would:

```
bob = User.find(7) # => #<User:0x2391234 ... >
bob.address        # => #<Address:0x238eaac @attributes={...}>

frank = User.find(3)      # =>
 #<User:0x2576dc4 ... >
frank.create_address(...) # =>
 #<Address:0x2576d74 @attributes={...}>
```

Validations

How many of us have had the experience of spending hours upon hours creating form validators, whether they are Java-Script or server-side validation. I know I have, and one of the reasons I love Rails: adding validation to your models is as easy as adding one line of code.

Here are the available validators that are useable by the models:

validates_acceptance_of(*attr_names)

Encapsulates the pattern of wanting to validate the acceptance of a Terms of Service checkbox (or similar agreement).

Example:

```
class Person < ActiveRecord::Base
  validates_acceptance_of :terms_of_service, :message =>
  "must be abided"
end
```

Options:

message
> A custom error message (default is "must be accepted").

on
> Specifies when this validation is active (default is :save; other options are :create and :update).

accept
> Specifies the value that is considered accepted. The default value is a string "1", which makes it easy to relate to an HTML checkbox.

if
> Specifies a method, proc, or string to call to determine if the validation should occur. The method, proc, or string should return or evaluate to a **true** or **false** value.

validates_associated(*attr_names)
> Validates whether the associated object or objects are all valid themselves. Works with any kind of association:

> Example:

```
class Book < ActiveRecord::Base
  has_many :pages
  belongs_to :library

  validates_associated :pages, :library
end
```

Options:

on
> Specifies when this validation is active (default is :save; other options are :create and :update).

if
> Specifies a method, proc, or string to call to determine if the validation should occur. The method, proc, or string should return or evaluate to a **true** or **false** value.

```
validates_confirmation_of(*attr_names)
```
Encapsulates the pattern of wanting to validate a password or email address field with a confirmation.

Example:

```
# Model
class Person < ActiveRecord::Base
  validates_confirmation_of :user_name, :password
  validates_confirmation_of :email_address, :message =>
    "should match confirmation"
end

# View
<%= password_field "person", "password" %>
<%= password_field "person", "password_confirmation" %>
```

The person has to already have a password attribute (a column in the people table), but the `password_confirma tion` is virtual. It exists only as an in-memory variable for validating the password. This check is performed only if `password_confirmation` is not `nil` and, by default, on save.

Options:

message

A custom error message (default is "doesn't match confirmation").

on

Specifies when this validation is active (default is `:save`; other options are `:create` and `:update`).

if

Specifies a method, proc, or string to call to determine if the validation should occur. The method, proc, or string should return or evaluate to a `true` or `false` value.

```
validates_each(*attrs) {|record, attr, value| ...}
```
Validates each attribute against a block.

Example:

```
class Person < ActiveRecord::Base
  validates_each :first_name, :last_name do
    |record, attr, value|
    record.errors.add attr, 'starts with z.'
      if value[0] == ?z
```

```
        end
    end
```

Options:

on

> Specifies when this validation is active (default is :save; other options are :create and :update).

allow_nil

> Skips validation if attribute is nil.

if

> Specifies a method, proc, or string to call to determine if the validation should occur. The method, proc, or string should return or evaluate to a true or false value.

validates_exclusion_of(*attr_names)

> Validates that the value of the specified attribute is not in a particular enumerable object.

Example:

```
class Person < ActiveRecord::Base
  validates_exclusion_of :role, :in => %w( admin superuser ),
    :message => "Go away. You should not be here."
  validates_exclusion_of :age, :in => 0..17,
    :message => "This site is only for ages 18 and over."
end
```

Options:

in

> An enumerable object of items that the value shouldn't be part of.

message

> A custom error message (default is "is reserved").

allow_nil

> If set to true, skips this validation if the attribute is null (default is false).

if

> Specifies a method, proc, or string to call to determine if the validation should occur. The method,

proc, or string should return or evaluate to a **true** or
false value.

validates_format_of(*attr_names)

Validates whether the value of the specified attribute is of
the correct form by matching it against the regular expression provided.

Example:

```
class Person < ActiveRecord::Base
  validates_format_of :email, :with =>
  /^([^@\s]+)@((?:[-a-z0-9]+\.)+[a-z]{2,})$/i, :on => :create
end
```

A regular expression must be provided or an exception
will be raised.

Options:

message

A custom error message (default is "is invalid").

with

The regular expression used to validate the format
with. (Note: this must be supplied!)

on

Specifies when this validation is active (default
is :save; other options are :create and :update).

if

Specifies a method, proc, or string to call to determine if the validation should occur. The method,
proc, or string should return or evaluate to a **true** or
false value.

validates_inclusion_of(*attr_names)

Validates whether the value of the specified attribute is
available in a particular enumerable object.

Example:

```
class Person < ActiveRecord::Base
  validates_inclusion_of :gender, :in => %w( M F ),
  :message => "Are you an alien then?"
  validates_inclusion_of :age, :in => 0..99
end
```

Options:

in

> An enumerable object of available items.

message

> Specifies a customer error message (default is "is not included in the list").

allow_nil

> If set to **true**, skips this validation if the attribute is null (default is **false**).

if

> Specifies a method, proc or string to call to determine if the validation should occur. The method, proc, or string should return or evaluate to a **true** or **false** value.

validates_length_of(*attrs)

> Validates that the specified attribute matches the length restrictions supplied. Only one option can be used at a time.
>
> Example:

```
class Person < ActiveRecord::Base
  validates_length_of :first_name, :maximum => 30
  validates_length_of :last_name, :maximum => 30, :message=>
   "must be less than %d characters"
  validates_length_of :fax, :in => 7..32, :allow_nil => true
  validates_length_of :username, :within => 6..20, :too_long =>
   "is too long",
   :too_short -> "is too short"
end
```

Options:

minimum

> The minimum size of the attribute.

maximum

> The maximum size of the attribute.

is

> The exact size of the attribute.

within

A range specifying the minimum and maximum size of the attribute.

in

A synonym (or alias) for :within.

allow_nil

Attribute may be nil; skip validation.

too_long

The error message if the attribute goes over the maximum (default is "is too long (maximum is %d characters)").

too_short

The error message if the attribute goes under the minimum (default is "is too short (min is %d characters)").

wrong_length

The error message if using the :is method and the attribute is the wrong size (default is "is the wrong length (should be %d characters)").

message

The error message to use for a :minimum, :maximum, or :is violation. An alias of the appropriate too_long/too_short/wrong_length message.

on

Specifies when this validation is active (default is :save; other options are :create and :update).

if

Specifies a method, proc or string to call to determine if the validation should occur. The method, proc, or string should return or evaluate to a true or false value.

validates_numericality_of(*attr_names)

Validates whether the value of the specified attribute is numeric by trying to convert it to a float with Kernel.Float (if integer is set to false) or applying it to the regular expression /^[+\-]?\d+$/ (if integer is set to true).

Example:

```
class Person < ActiveRecord::Base
  validates_numericality_of :age, :on => :create
end
```

Options:

message
> A custom error message (default is "is not a number").

on
> Specifies when this validation is active (default is :save; other options are :create and :update).

only_integer
> Specifies whether the value has to be an integer, e.g., an integral value (default is false).

allow_nil
> If set to true, skips this validation if the attribute is null (default is false).

if
> Specifies a method, proc, or string to call to determine if the validation should occur. The method, proc, or string should return or evaluate to a true or false value.

validates_presence_of(*attr_names)
> Validates that the specified attributes are not blank (as defined by Object#blank?). Happens by default on save.

Example:

```
class Person < ActiveRecord::Base
  validates_presence_of :first_name
end
```

The first_name attribute must be in the object and it cannot be blank.

Options:

message
> A custom error message (default is "can't be blank").

on
> Specifies when this validation is active (default is :save; other options are :create and :update).

if
> Specifies a method, proc, or string to call to determine if the validation should occur. The method, proc, or string should return or evaluate to a true or false value.

validates_size_of(*attrs)
> Alias for validates_length_of.

validates_uniqueness_of(*attr_names)
> Validates whether the value of the specified attributes are unique across the system.

> Example:

```
class Person < ActiveRecord::Base
  validates_uniqueness_of :username, :scope => :account_id
end
```

> It can also validate whether the value of the specified attributes are unique based on multiple scope parameters, for example, making sure that a teacher can only be on the schedule once per semester for a particular class:

```
class TeacherSchedule < ActiveRecord::Base
  validates_uniqueness_of :book_title, :scope =>
  [:semester_id, :class_id]
end
```

> When the record is created, a check is performed to make sure that no record exists in the database with the given value for the specified attribute (that maps to a column). When the record is updated, the same check is made but disregarding the record itself.

Options:

message

>A custom error message (default is "has already been taken").

scope

>One or more columns by which to limit the scope of the uniqueness constraint.

if

>Specifies a method, proc, or string to call to determine if the validation should occur. The method, proc, or string should return or evaluate to a `true` or `false` value.

Named Scope

In Rails 2.1, Nick Kallen's `has_finder` plugin (*http://pivots.piv otallabs.com/users/nick/blog*) became part of Rails in the form of `named_scope`. The `named_scope` method makes performing finds on models very convenient. For example:

```
# models/user.rb

class User < ActiveRecord::Base
  named_scope :active, :conditions => {:active => true}
  named_scope :inactive, :conditions => {:active => false}
  named_scope :recent, lambda { { :conditions =>
    ['created_at > ?', 1.week.ago] } }
end

# Standard usage
User.active
# same as User.find(:all, :conditions => {:active => true})
User.inactive
# same as User.find(:all, :conditions => {:active => false})
User.recent
# same as User.find(:all, :conditions => ['created_at > ?', 1.week.ago])

# They're nest-able too!
User.active.recent
 # same as:
 # User.with_scope(:conditions => {:active => true}) do
 #   User.find(:all, :conditions => ['created_at > ?', 1.week.ago])
 # end
```

Passing arguments

More complex finds can be done using lambda to pass in arguments to your named scopes at runtime.

Example:

```
class User < ActiveRecord::Base
  named_scope :registered,
  lambda { |time_ago| { :conditions =>
  ['created_at > ?', time_ago] }
end

User.registered 7.days.ago
# same as User.find(:all, :conditions =>
['created_at > ?', 7.days.ago])
```

Named scope extensions

Scopes can also be extended, similar to association extensions (*http://api.rubyonrails.org/classes/ActiveRecord/Associations/ClassMethods.html*).

Example:

```
class User < ActiveRecord::Base
  named_scope :inactive, :conditions => {:active => false} do
    def activate
      each { |i| i.update_attribute(:active, true) }
    end
  end
end

# Re-activate all inactive users
User.inactive.activate
```

Anonymous scopes

You can also pass around scopes as first-class objects using scope (a named scoped provided to you for free) as a way to build hairy queries on the fly.

Example:

```
# Store named scopes
active = User.scoped(:conditions => {:active => true})
recent = User.scoped(:conditions => ['created_at > ?', 7.days.ago])

# Which can be combined
recent_active = recent.active
```

```
# And operated upon
recent_active.each { |u| ... }
```

For more information on named_scope, visit Ryan Daigle's blog entry at *http://ryandaigle.com/articles/2008/3/24/what-s-new -in-edge-rails-has-finder-functionality*.

CRUD: Create, Read, Update, Delete

All databases have four common functions: CREATE, READ, UPDATE, and DELETE rows in tables. This is commonly referenced as CRUD. Rails via ActiveRecord makes these operations very simple to use.

Create

There are two ways to add a record into the database using the associated model. The first is using the .new method.

When using .new, the method accepts either a hash or a block as the parameter. It works like this:

```
movie = Movie.new(:title => "Twilight of the Cockroaches",
                  :rating => "Unrated")
movie.save # Saves the record
```

You can also use block initialization:

```
movie = Movie.new do |m|
  m.title = "Twilight of the Cockroaches"
  m.rating = "Unrated"
end
movie.save
```

You can also do it the simple way:

```
movie = Movie.new
movie.title = "Twilight of the Cockroaches"
movie.rating = "Unrated"
movie.save
```

On all the previous examples, the method .save is called at the end. This is what performs the commit to the database (if validation passes) and returns the model object. If the save fails under validations, the unsaved object is still returned.

Another method used to add records into the database is .create. This method takes the same parameters as .new but commits it to the database instantly—if the validation permits it—and returns it. If the save fails under validations, the unsaved object is still returned.

Example:

```
movie = Movie.create(:title => "Twilight of the Cockroaches",
                     :rating => "Unrated")
```

You can also use the exclamation mark (!) to force an exception if the **save** or **create** methods fail.

```
# raises an ActiveRecord::RecordInvalid exception
movie = Movie.create!(:title => nil, :rating = "Unrated")
movie = Movie.new.save!
```

Read

The method in which ActiveRecord reads data from the database is performed using the **find** command. There are several shortcuts that can be used when finding records:

find([id])

> This can either be a specific ID (1), a list of IDs (1, 5, 6), or an array of IDs ([5, 6, 10]). If no record can be found for all of the listed IDs, then **RecordNotFound** will be raised. For example:
>
> ```
> Movie.find(1) # Returns the movie with the id of 1
> ```

find([id])

> This will return the first record matching the provided options. These options can either be specific conditions or merely an order. If no record can be matched, **nil** is returned:
>
> ```
> Movie.find(:first, :order => :title)
> # Returns the first movie ordered by title
> Movie.first # Returns the first movie ordered by id
> ```

find([id])

> This will return all the records matching the provided options. If no records are found, an empty array is returned:

```
Movie.find(:all, :conditions => { :rating => "PG-13" },
                  :order => :title)
# Returns all PG-13 movies, ordered by title
Movie.all # Returns all movies ordered by id
```

All approaches listed above accept an option hash as their last parameter.

Options:

`:conditions`
> SQL conditions, typically following `where` in the SQL command.

`:order`
> Order in which results are to be sorted.

`:group`
> Groups the results by column.

`:limit`
> Maximum number of results to be returned.

`:offset`
> Offsets the results. So, at 5, it would skip the first 4 rows.

`:joins`
> Performs joins on SQL queries. The records will be returned read-only since they will have attributes that do not correspond to the table's columns. Pass `:readonly =>` `false` to override.

`:include`
> Performs a `LEFT OUTER JOIN` on the provided tables. The symbols named refer to already defined associations.

`:select`
> By default, this is `*`, as in `SELECT * FROM`, but can be changed to limit the returned columns to the specified ones.

`:readonly`
> Marks the returned records read-only so that they cannot be saved or updated.

Examples:

```
Movie.find(1)
# Returns the movie with the id of 1
Movie.find(1, 2, 6)
# Returns an array of objects with IDs in (1, 2, 6)
Movie.find([25, 49])
# returns an array of objects with IDs in (25, 49)

Movie.find(:first, :order => :title)
# Returns the first movie ordered by title
Movie.first
# Returns the first movie ordered by id
Movie.first(:conditions => ["rating = ?", "G"])
# Returns the first movie with a rating of 'G', ordered by id

Movie.find(:all, :conditions => { :rating => "PG-13" }, :order => :title)
# Returns all PG-13 movies, ordered by title
Movie.all
# Returns all movies ordered by id
Movie.find(:all, :group => "rating")
# Returns all movies grouped by rating
Movie.find(:all, :include => [:comments])
# Returns all movies with associated comments
Movie.find(:all, :offset => 10, :limit => 10)
# Returns the 11th through 20th movies, ordered by id
```

To perform a query from a custom SQL statement, you can use
`find_by_sql`.

Examples:

```
Movie.find_by_sql "SELECT m.*, c.body FROM movies m, comments c " +
                  "WHERE m.id = c.movie_id"
Movie.find_by_sql ["SELECT * FROM movies WHERE rating = ?", "R"]
```

Dynamic attribute-based finders are a cleaner way of getting
(and/or creating) objects by simple queries without turning to
SQL.

Examples:

```
Person.find_by_user_name("cavneb")
Person.find_or_create_by_username("cavneb", :first_name => "Eric",
                                           :last_name => "Berry")
```

For more information on ActiveRecord methods, go to *http://
api.rubyonrails.org/classes/ActiveRecord/Base.html*.

Update

ActiveRecord uses four methods to perform updates to the database:

`update(id, attributes)`
> Finds the record from the passed ID, instantly saves it with the passed attributes (if the validation permits it), and returns it. If the save fails under validations, the unsaved object is still returned.
>
> The arguments may also be given as arrays, in which case, the update method is called for each pair of IDs and attributes, and an array of objects is returned.
>
> Example of updating one record:
> ```
> Movie.update(25, {:title => 'Seven Samurai', :genre =>
>   'Classics'})
> ```
>
> Example of updating multiple records:
> ```
> movies = { 1 => { "rating" => "PG" }, 2 => { "title" =>
>   "Sixth Sense"} }
> Movie.update(movies.keys, movies.values)
> ```

`update_all(updates, conditions = nil)`
> Updates all records and returns an integer with the number of rows updated.
>
> Example:
> ```
> Movie.update_all "in_stock = true"
> ```

`update_attribute(name, value)`
> Updates a single database record. This method does not fall subject to model validation, meaning that an attribute can be updated without the object being valid.
>
> Example:
> ```
> movie = Movie.find(:first) # Returns first movie in the table
> movie.update_attribute("rating", "G")
> ```

`update_attributes(attributes)`
> Updates all the attributes from a hash and saves the record. If the object is invalid, the saving will fail and

`false` will be returned. This is commonly used when updating a model object from a form post.

Example:
```
params = { :movie => { :title =>
  "When Harry Met Sally" }}

movie = Movie.find(16)
person.update_attributes(params[:movie])
```

Delete

ActiveRecord has four methods that delete database records:

delete(id)

    Deletes the record with the given ID without instantiating
an object first. If an array of IDs is provided, all of them
are deleted.

    Examples:
```
# Delete a person by id
Person.delete(15)

# Delete an array of people by id
Person.delete([4,8,15,16,23,42])
```

delete_all(conditions = nil)

    Deletes all the records that match the condition without
instantiating the objects first.

    Examples:
```
Person.delete_all "last_name = 'Test'"

# Delete all table rows
Person.delete_all
```

destroy(id)

    Destroys the record with the given ID by instantiating the
object and calling **destroy** (all the callbacks are then triggered). If an array of IDs is provided, all of them are
destroyed.

    Example:
```
# Destroy a movie by id
Movie.destroy(8) # Performs all callbacks prior to delete
```

```
destroy_all(conditions = nil)
```
Destroys the objects for all the records that match the condition by instantiating each object and calling the **destroy** method.

Example:

```
Session.destroy_all "created_at < '2008-07-21'"
```

TIP

The delete and delete_all_methods are not commonly used, as they do not perform any of the callbacks. Best practice is to use **destroy** and destroy_all.

Conditions

Many of the previously mentioned CRUD commands can be provided with :conditions. The conditions are the WHERE portion of the SQL query.

The :conditions parameter can be either a regular string or a collection of values.

Examples:

```
# Find using a string conditions parameter
Book.find(:first, :conditions => "title = 'Ruby Pocket Reference'
  AND author = 'Michael Fitzgerald'")

# Find using a collection of values
Comment.delete_all(:conditions => ["author_id = ?", author_id])
Book.find(:first, :conditions => ["title = ? AND author = ?",
 "Ruby Pocket Reference", "Michael Fitzgerald"])
```

Dirty objects

With the release of Rails 2.1, the ability to track whether your ActiveRecord objects have been modified became a lot easier with the dirty object functionality. Visit Ryan Daigle's blog at *http://ryandaigle.com/articles/2008/3/31/what-s-new-in-edge -rails-dirty-objects* for a great example of these new features.

```
article = Article.find(:first)
article.changed?  #=> false

# Track changes to individual attributes with
# attr_name_changed? accessor
article.title  #=> "Title"
article.title = "New Title"
article.title_changed? #=> true

# Access previous value with attr_name_was accessor
article.title_was  #=> "Title"

# See both previous and current value with attr_name_change accessor
article.title_change  #=> ["Title", "New Title"]
```

Beyond the clever attribute-based accessor methods, you can also query to an object directly for its list of all changed attributes. (Continuing from the previous example):

```
# Get a list of changed attributes
article.changed  #=> ['title']

# Get the hash of changed attributes and their previous and
current values
article.changes  #=> { 'title' => ["Title", "New Title"] }
```

Once you save a dirty object, it clears out its changed state tracking and is once again considered unchanged:

```
article.changed?  #=> true
article.save       #=> true
article.changed?  #=> false
```

If you're going to be modifying an attribute outside of the attr= writer, you can use attr_name_will_change! to tell the object to be aware of the change:

```
article = Article.find(:first)
article.title_will_change!
article.title.upcase!
article.title_change  #=> ['Title', 'TITLE']
```

Partial updates

In lock-step with the recent dirty objects functionality comes the ability of ActiveRecord models to perform partial updates, which saves only the attributes that have been modified on updates. For example:

```
article = Article.find(:first)
article.title    #=> "Title"
```

```
article.subject  #=> "Edge Rails"

# Update one of the attributes
article.title = "New Title"

# And only that updated attribute is persisted to the db
article.save
  #=>  "UPDATE articles SET title = 'New Title' WHERE id = 1"
```

To disable this functionality, set `partial_updates = false` for each model you wish not to take advantage of partial updates. To disable this system-wide, add this line to your *environment.rb* or, better yet, in a *config/initializer*:

```
ActiveRecord::Base.partial_updates = false
```

Database Configurations

Rails uses a database abstraction layer called ActiveRecord. Using ActiveRecord, the developer can create applications that interact with SQLite (2 and 3), MySQL, PostgreSQL, SQLite, Microsoft SQL Server, and Oracle (all supported databases except DB2) without messing with SQL nuances between the database types.

In Rails 2.1, SQLite (*http://www.sqlite.org*) is the default database. The database connection settings can be found in *config/database.yml.*

```
development: # Development environment
  adapter: sqlite3
  database: db/development.sqlite3
  timeout: 5000

test: # Test environment
  adapter: sqlite3
  database: db/test.sqlite3
  timeout: 5000

production: # Production environment
  adapter: sqlite3
  database: db/production.sqlite3
  timeout: 5000
```

The following are some examples of different database configurations in the *database.yml* file.

MySQL

```
adapter: mysql
encoding: utf8
database: test-mysql_development
username: dbuser
password: dbpswd
socket: /tmp/mysql.sock # Change if needed
```

PostgreSQL

```
adapter: postgresql
encoding: unicode
database: test-postgres_development
username: dbuser
password: dbpswd
host: localhost
port: 5432
```

Oracle

```
adapter: oracle
database: test-oracle_development
username: dbuser
password: dbpswd
prefetch_rows: 100      # optional
cursor_sharing: similar # optional
```

If using an Oracle database, Rails requires Ruby/OCI8, found at *http://rubyforge.org/projects/ruby-oci8*.

Microsoft SQL Server

Starting with Rails 2.1, the ActiveRecord SQL Server adapter is no longer included by default and must be installed separately:

```
gem install activerecord-sqlserver-adapter
  --source=http://gems.rubyonrails.org
```

For instructions on how to install and use Microsoft SQL Server with Rails, visit *http://wiki.rubyonrails.org/rails/pages/HowtoConnectToMicrosoftSQLServer*.

Using Multiple Database Configurations

Let's say that we have an application that we want to communicate with Salesforce (*http://www.salesforce.com*) via the

ActiveSalesforce gem (*http://activesfdc.rubyforge.org*). You would do the following:

1. Install the `activesalesforce` gem.

2. Create a model to represent the Salesforce table, i.e., Lead, by creating the file *app/models/lead.rb*.

3. Add the new database settings to your *database.yml* file:

```
salesforce:
  adapter: activesalesforce
  url: https://www.salesforce.com
  username: xxxxxxx
  password: xxxxxxx
```

4. Modify *app/models/lead.rb* and set the connection:

```
class Lead < ActiveRecord::Base
  Lead.establish_connection(
    YAML.load(
      File.open(
        File.join(RAILS_ROOT,"config/database.yml"),"r")
      )["salesforce"]
    )
end
```

5. Restart your application.

Now when you do any ActiveRecord queries with the Lead model, the `salesforce` database connection will be used.

Action Controllers

Action controllers or *controllers* are the entry points of a web request. They are made up of one or more actions that are executed on requests and then either render a template or redirect to another action. An *action* is defined as a public method on the controller, which will automatically be made accessible to the web server through Rails routes. For more on Action controllers, go to *http://api.rubyonrails.org/classes/ActionControl ler/Base.html*.

Here is my MainController from my ClearPlay Movie List iPhone webapp (*http://clearplaymovies.mobi*):

```
class MainController < ApplicationController

  def index
  end

  def movies
    @letter = params[:id]
    if @letter == "other"
      criteria = []
      ("A".."Z").each do |letter|
        criteria << "title not like '#{letter}%'"
      end
      @movies = Movie.find(:all, :conditions => criteria.join(' and '),
        :order => :title)
    else
      @movies = Movie.find(:all, :conditions => "title like '#{@letter}%'",
        :order => :title)
    end
  end

end
```

By default, actions render a template in the *app/views* directory
that corresponds to the name of the controller and action after
executing code in the action. For example, the index action of
the MainController here would render the template
app/views/movies/index.html.erb.

Requests

Requests are processed by the ActionController framework by
extracting the value of the *action* key in the request parameters.
This value should hold the name of the action to be performed.
Once the action has been identified, the remaining request parameters, the session (if one is available), and the full request
with all the HTTP headers are made available to the action
through instance variables. Then the action is performed.

The full request object is available with the request accessor
and is primarily used to query for HTTP headers. These queries
are made by accessing the environment hash, like this:

```
def server_ip
  location = request.env["SERVER_ADDR"]
  render :text => "This server hosted at #{location}"
end
```

Parameters

All request parameters, whether they come from a GET or POST request or from the URL, are available through the params method, which returns a hash. For example, an action performed through */weblog/list?category=All&limit=5* will include { "category" => "All", "limit" => 5 } in params.

It's also possible to construct multidimensional parameter hashes by specifying keys using brackets, such as:

```
<input type="text" name="post[name]" value="Eric Berry">
<input type="text" name="post[address]" value="1066 N 300 W">
```

A request stemming from a form holding these inputs will include { "post" => { "name" => "Eric Berry", "address" => "1066 N 300 W" } }. If the address input had been named post[address][street], the params would have included { "post" => { "address" => { "street" => "1066 N 300 W" } } }. There's no limit to the depth of the nesting.

Sessions

Sessions allows you to store objects in between requests. This is useful for objects that are not yet ready to be persisted, such as a Signup object constructed in a multipaged process, or objects that don't change much and are needed all the time, such as a User object for a system that requires a login. The session should not be used, however, as a cache for objects where it's likely they could be changed unknowingly. It's usually too much work to keep it all synchronized—something at which databases already excel.

You can place objects in the session using the session method, which accesses a hash:

```
session[:person] = Person.authenticate(user_name, password)
```

It can be retrieved again through the same hash:

```
Hello #{session[:person].first_name}
```

For removing objects from the session, you can either assign a single key to nil, like `session[:person] = nil`, or you can remove the entire session with `reset_session`.

TIP

It is not recommended to store objects into the session other than simple objects (e.g., string or int). With some sessions, the limit of data is 4k, and also the integrity of the object being stored may not be retained.

CookieStore sessions are stored in a browser cookie that's cryptographically signed but unencrypted by default. This prevents the user from tampering with the session but also allows him to see its contents. This cookie-based session store is used by default. Sessions typically contain at most a `user_id` and flash message, which fit within the 4K cookie size limit. Cookie-based sessions are dramatically faster than the alternatives.

CAUTION

Do not put secret information in a CookieStore session!

Other options for session storage are:

ActiveRecordStore

ActiveRecordStore sessions are stored in your database, which works better than PStore with multiple app servers and, unlike CookieStore, hides your session contents from the user. To use ActiveRecordStore, set:

```
config.action_controller.session_store = :active_record_store
```

in your *environment.rb* and run `rake db:sessions:create`.

MemCacheStore

MemCacheStore sessions are stored as entries in your memcached cache. Set the session store type in *environment.rb*:

```
# This assumes that memcached has been installed and
configured properly.
# See the MemCacheStore docs for more information.

config.action_controller.session_store = :mem_cache_store
```

Responses

Each action results in a response, which holds the headers and document to be sent to the user's browser. The actual response object is generated automatically through the use of renders and redirects and requires no user intervention.

Renders

ActionController sends content to the user by using one of five rendering methods. The most versatile and common is the rendering of a template. Included in the ActionPack is the ActionView, which enables rendering of ERb templates. It's automatically configured. The controller passes objects to the view by assigning instance variables:

```
def show
  @post = Post.find(params[:id])
end
```

These are then automatically available to the view:

```
Title: <%= @post.title %>
```

You don't have to rely on the automated rendering. Particularly actions that could result in the rendering of different templates will use the manual rendering methods:

```
def search
  @results = Search.find(params[:query])
  case @results
    when 0 then render :action => "no_results"
    when 1 then render :action => "show"
    when 2..10 then render :action -> "show_many"
  end
end
```

Redirects

Redirects are used to move from one action to another. For example, after a create action, which stores a blog entry to a database, we might like to show the user the new entry. Because we're following good DRY (Don't Repeat Yourself) principles, we're going to reuse (and redirect to) a show action that we'll assume has already been created. The code might look like this:

```
def create
  @entry = Entry.new(params[:entry])
  if @entry.save
    # The entry was saved correctly, redirect to show
    redirect_to :action => 'show', :id => @entry.id
  else
    # things didn't go so well, do something else
  end
end
```

In this case, after saving our new entry to the database, the user is redirected to the show method, which is then executed.

Calling Multiple Redirects or Renders

An action may contain only a single render or a single redirect. Attempting to try to do either again will result in a `DoubleRenderError`:

```
def do_something
  redirect_to :action => "elsewhere"
  render :action => "overthere" # raises DoubleRenderError
end
```

If you need to redirect on the condition of something, then be sure to add **and return** to halt execution:

```
def do_something
  redirect_to(:action => "elsewhere") and return if monkeys.nil?
  render :action => "overthere" # won't be called unless monkeys is nil
end
```

Views

ActionView templates can be written in three ways. If the template file has an *.erb* (or *.rhtml*) extension then it uses a mixture of ERb (included in Ruby) and HTML. If the template file has a *.builder* (or *.rxml*) extension, then Jim Weirich's `Builder::XmlMarkup` (*http://api.rubyonrails.org/classes/Builder/ XmlMarkup.html*) library is used. If the template file has a *.rjs* extension, then it will use *ActionView::Helpers::Prototype- Helper::JavaScriptGenerator*.

Using Variables with ERb

You trigger ERb using embeddings, such as <% %>, <% -%>, and <%= %>. The <%= %> tag set is used when you want output. Consider the following loop for names:

```
<b>Names of all the people</b>
<% for person in @people %>
  Name: <%= person.name %><br/>
<% end %>
```

The loop is set up in regular embedding tags <% %>, and the name is written using the output embedding tag <%- %>. This is not just a usage suggestion. Regular output functions like `print` or `puts` won't work with ERb templates. So, this would be wrong:

```
Hi, Mr. <% puts "load" %>
```

If you absolutely must write from within a function, you can use the TextHelper `concat`.

<%- and -%> suppress leading and trailing whitespace, including the trailing newline, and can be used interchangeably with <% and %>.

Layouts and Templates

One of the great benefits of using the Rails framework is the ability to use layouts. A layout defines the surroundings of an

HTML page. It's the place to define the common look and feel of your final output. Layout files reside in *app/views/layouts*.

respond_to

You can assign a response to render differently based on the format or suffix of the request. Without web service support, an action that collects the data for displaying a list of people might look something like this:

```
def index
  @people = Person.all
end
```

Here's the same action, with web service support built-in:

```
def index
  @people = Person.find(:all)

  respond_to do |format|
    format.html
    format.js   { render :layout => false }
    # Don't render a layout if .js file
    format.xml { render :xml => @people.to_xml }
    # Render the response using the XML builder
    format.json { render :json => @people.to_json }
    # Render the response using the to_json method
  end
end
```

Using different suffixes in my URL gives me a different result. For example, if I were to go to *http://localhost:3000/peo ple.html*, I would see the standard response, as shown in Example 1-1.

Example 1-1. people.html

```
<!DOCTYPE html PUBLIC "-//W3C//DTD XHTML 1.0 Transitional//EN"
    "http://www.w3.org/TR/xhtml1/DTD/xhtml1-transitional.dtd">

<html xmlns="http://www.w3.org/1999/xhtml" xml:lang="en" lang="en">
<head>
  <meta http-equiv="content-type" content="text/html;charset=UTF-8" />
  <title>Example</title>
</head>
<body>

<table>
  <tr>
    <th>First Name</th>
```

```
      <th>Last Name</th>
      <th>Email</th>
    </tr>
    <tr>
      <td>Dave</td>
      <td>Anderson</td>
      <td>david.anderson@oreilly.com</td>
    </tr>
</table>

</body>
</html>
```

If I were to go to the same URL but instead of using .html, used .xml, I would get a different response altogether, as shown in Example 1-2.

Example 1-2. people.xml

```
<?xml version="1.0" encoding="UTF-8"?>
<people type="array">
    <person>
    <first-name>Dave</first-name>
    <last-name>Anderson</last-name>
    <id type="integer">1</id>
    <email>david.anderson@oreilly.com</email>
    </person>
</people>
```

Using .json, I would get what's shown in Example 1-3.

Example 1-3. people.json

```
[{"person": {"id": 1, "first_name": "Dave", "last_name": "Anderson",
            "email": "david.anderson@oreilly.com"}}]
```

Using custom formats with respond_to

With the power of Rails, you are even able to create your own formats. Let's assume we wanted to create an application that has a separate layout and view for iPhone users:

1. We'll start off by registering the iphone mime type in *config/initializers/mime_types*:

        Mime::Type.register_alias "text/html", :iphone

2. Now we can add a new view specifically for iPhone users (*app/views/people/index.iphone.erb*):

```
<ul>
  <% @people.each do |person| -%>
    <li><%= "#{person.first_name} #{person.last_name}" %>
    </li>
  <% end -%>
</ul>
```

3. We can also create a layout specific to the iPhone style guide (*app/views/layouts/iphone.html.erb*):

```
<!DOCTYPE html PUBLIC "-//W3C//DTD XHTML 1.0 Strict//EN"
    "http://www.w3.org/TR/xhtml1/DTD/xhtml1-strict.dtd">
<html xmlns="http://www.w3.org/1999/xhtml">
  <head>
    <meta http-equiv="content-type" content="text/html;
    charset=utf-8" />
    <meta name="viewport" content="width=device-width,
    user-scalable=no" />
    <link rel="apple-touch-icon" href="/images/myapp.png">
    <title>My App</title>
    <link rel = "stylesheet" href =
    "/stylesheets/EdgeToEdge.css" />
  </head>
  <body>
    <h1 id="pageTitle">My App</h1>

    <%= yield %>

  </body>
</html>
```

4. Now add the iphone format to the respond_to block as shown in the previous section:

```
def index
  @people = Person.find(:all)

  respond_to do |format|
    format.html
    format.js    { render :layout => false }
    # Don't render a layout
    format.xml   { render :xml => @people.to_xml }
    # Render using the XML builder
    format.json  { render :json => @people.to_json }
    # Render using the to_json method
    format.iphone
    # Render *.iphone.erb
  end
end
```

5. Now you should see the new format when you go to *http://localhost:3000/people.iphone*:

```
<!DOCTYPE html PUBLIC "-//W3C//DTD XHTML 1.0 Strict//EN"
    "http://www.w3.org/TR/xhtml1/DTD/xhtml1-strict.dtd">
<html xmlns="http://www.w3.org/1999/xhtml">
  <head>
    <meta http-equiv="content-type" content="text/html;
    charset=utf-8" />
    <meta name="viewport" content="width=device-width,
    user-scalable=no" />
    <link rel="apple-touch-icon" href="/images/myapp.png">
    <title>My App</title>
    <link rel = "stylesheet" href =
    "/stylesheets/EdgeToEdge.css" />
  </head>

  <body>
    <h1 id="pageTitle">My App</h1>

    <ul>
      <li>Dave Anderson</li>
    </ul>

  </body>
</html>
```

Builder

Builder templates are a more programmatic alternative to ERb.
They are especially useful for generating XML content. A
Builder::XmlMarkup object named xml is automatically made
available to templates with a *.builder* extension.

Here are some basic examples.

```
xml.div("contents")
# => <div>contents</div>
xml.h3 { xml.strong("h3 & strong") }
# => <h3><strong>h3 &amp; strong</strong></h3>
xml.a("Partner Fusion", "href"=>"http://partnerfusion.com")
# => <a href="http://partnerfusion.com">Partner Fusion</a>
```

Any method with a block will be treated as an XML markup
tag with nested markup in the block. For example, the
following:

```
xml.div {
  xml.h1(@person.name)
  xml.p(@person.bio)
}
```

would produce something like:

```
<div>
  <h1>Ryan Williams</h1>
  <p>CEO of Partner Fusion.</p>
</div>
```

As another example, if I wanted to create a simple XML feed for an action that renders a movie list, I could add a format responder to the action:

```
# apps/controllers/movies_controller.rb

...
def movies
  @movies = Movie.all
  respond_to do |format|
    format.html
    format.xml
  end
end
```

Then I would add a new *.builder* file to display the results:

```
# apps/views/movies/movies.xml.builder

xml.instruct! :xml, :version=>"1.0", :encoding=>"UTF-8"
xml.movies do
  @movies.each do |movie|
    xml.movie(movie.title)
  end
end
```

Visit *http://builder.rubyforge.org* for more Builder documentation. Also, for an in-depth example of how to create XML with Ruby and Builder, read Michael Fitzgerald's blog at *http://www.xml.com/pub/a/2006/01/04/creating-xml-with-ruby-and-builder.html*.

JavaScriptGenerator

JavaScriptGenerator templates end in *.rjs*. Unlike conventional templates, which are used to render the results of an action, these templates generate instructions on how to modify an already rendered page. This makes it easy to modify multiple elements on your page in one declarative Ajax response. Actions with these templates are called in the background with Ajax and make updates to the page where the request originated.

An instance of the JavaScriptGenerator object-named page is automatically made available to your template, which is implicitly wrapped in an ActionView::Helpers::Prototype-Helper `update_page` block.

When an *.rjs* action is called with `link_to_remote`, the generated JavaScript is automatically evaluated.

Example:

```
link_to_remote :url => {:action => 'delete'}
```

The subsequently rendered *delete.rjs* might look like this:

```
page.replace_html  'sidebar', :partial => 'sidebar'
page.remove        "person-#{@person.id}"
page.visual_effect :highlight, 'user-list'
```

This refreshes the sidebar, removes a person element, and highlights the user list.

Using subtemplates

Using subtemplates allows you to sidestep tedious replication and extract common display structures in shared templates. The classic example is the use of a header and footer (even though the ActionPack way would be to use layouts):

```
<%= render "shared/header" %>
something really specific and terrific
<%= render "shared/footer" %>
```

As you see, we use the output embeddings for the render methods. The render call itself will just return a string holding the result of the rendering. The output embedding writes it to the current template.

But you don't have to restrict yourself to static includes. Templates can share variables among themselves by using instance variables that are defined using the regular embedding tags, like this:

```
<% @page_title = "A Wonderful Hello" %>
<%= render "shared/header" %>
```

Now the header can pick up on the `@page_title` variable and use it for outputting a title tag:

```
<title><%= @page_title %></title>
```

However, if you need more control over your included content, partials may be a better solution.

Partials

Partials are small collections of code that can be included in any part of a view, or even rendered from the controller. They usually take at least one object as a parameter but can be customized to take any amount. Partials are named with a _ prefix to separate them from regular templates that could be rendered on their own.

In a template for *Advertiser* **account**, we could have:

```
<%= render :partial => "account" %>
```

This would render *advertiser/_account.html.erb* and pass the instance variable **@account** in as a local variable account to the template for display.

In another template for *Advertiser* **buy**, we could have:

```
<%= render :partial => "account", :locals => { :account => @buyer } %>

<% for ad in @advertisements %>
  <%= render :partial => "ad", :locals => { :ad => ad } %>
<% end %>
```

This would first render *advertiser/_account.html.erb* with *@buyer* passed in as the local variable account, then render *advertiser/_ad.html.erb* and pass the local variable ad to the template for display.

Rendering a collection of partials

The example of partial use describes a familiar pattern where a template needs to iterate over an array and render a subtemplate for each of the elements. This pattern has been implemented as a single method that accepts an array and renders a partial by the same name as the elements contained within. So the previous three-lined example can be rewritten with a single line:

```
<%= render :partial => "ad", :collection => @advertisements %>
```

This will render *advertiser/_ad.html.erb* and pass the local variable ad to the template for display. An iteration counter will automatically be made available to the template with a name of the form *partial_name_counter*. In the case of the previous example, the template would be fed *ad_counter*.

NOTE

Due to backward compatibility concerns, the collection can't be one of hashes. Normally, you'd also just keep domain objects, like ActiveRecords, in there.

Rendering shared partials

Two controllers can share a set of partials and render them like this:

```
<%= render :partial => "advertisement/ad", :locals =>
  { :ad => @advertisement } %>
```

This will render the partial *advertisement/_ad.html.erb* regardless of which controller this is being called from.

Rendering partials with layouts

Partials can have their own layouts applied to them. These layouts are different than the ones that are specified globally for the entire action, but they work in a similar fashion. Imagine a list with two types of users:

```
<%# app/views/users/index.html.erb %>
Here's the administrator:
<%= render :partial => "user", :layout => "administrator", :locals =>
  { :user => administrator } %>

Here's the editor:
<%= render :partial => "user", :layout => "editor", :locals =>
  { :user => editor } %>

<%# app/views/users/_user.html.erb %>
Name: <%= user.name %>

<%# app/views/users/_administrator.html.erb %>
<div id="administrator">
```

```
  Budget: $<%= user.budget %>
  <%= yield %>
</div>

<%# app/views/users/_editor.html.erb %>
<div id="editor">
  Deadline: $<%= user.deadline %>
  <%= yield %>
</div>
```

This will return:

```
Here's the administrator:
<div id="administrator">
  Budget: $<%= user.budget %>
  Name: <%= user.name %>
</div>

Here's the editor:
<div id="editor">
  Deadline: $<%= user.deadline %>
  Name: <%= user.name %>
</div>
```

You can also apply a layout to a block within any template:

```
<% # app/views/users/_chief.html.erb %>
<% render(:layout => "administrator", :locals =>
  { :user => chief }) do %>
  Title: <%= chief.title %>
<% end %>
```

This will return:

```
<div id="administrator">
  Budget: $<%= user.budget %>
  Title: <%= chief.name %>
</div>
```

As you can see, the :locals hash is shared between both the
partial and its layout.

Caching

Caching is a cheap way of speeding up slow applications by
keeping the result of calculations, renderings, and database
calls around for subsequent requests. ActionController affords
you three approaches in varying levels of granularity: page
caching, action caching, and fragment caching.

Page caching

Page caching is an approach to caching where the entire action output is stored as an HTML file that the web server can serve without going through the ActionPack. This can be as much as 100 times faster than going through the process of dynamically generating the content. Unfortunately, this incredible speed-up is only available to stateless pages where all visitors are treated the same way. Content-management systems—including weblogs and wikis—have many pages that are a great fit for this approach, but account-based systems where people log in and manipulate their own data are often less likely candidates.

Specifying which actions to cache is done through the caches_page method:

```
class WeblogController < ActionController::Base
  caches_page :show, :new
end
```

This will generate cache files, such as *weblog/show/5* and *weblog/new*, that match the URLs used to trigger the dynamic generation. This is how the web server is able to pick up a cache file when it exists and otherwise let the request pass on to the ActionPack to generate it.

Expiration of the cache is handled by deleting the cached file, which results in a lazy regeneration approach where the cache is not restored before another hit is made against it. The API for doing so mimics the options from url_for and friends:

```
class WeblogController < ActionController::Base
  def update
    List.update(@params["list"]["id"], @params["list"])
    expire_page :action => "show", :id => @params["list"]["id"]
    redirect_to :action => "show", :id => @params["list"]["id"]
  end
end
```

Additionally, you can expire caches using *sweepers* that act on changes in the model to determine when a cache is supposed to be expired.

Setting the cache directory. The cache directory should be the document root for the web server and is set using `Base.page_cache_directory = "/document/root"`. For Rails, this directory has already been set to `RAILS_ROOT + "/public"`.

Setting the cache extension. By default, the cache extension is *.html*, which makes it easy for the cached files to be picked up by the web server. If you want something else, like *.php* or *.shtml*, just set `Base.page_cache_extension`.

Methods. The following are methods that can be used for page caching:

`cache_page(content = nil, options = {})`
> Manually caches the content in the key determined by options. If no content is provided, the contents of `@response.body` are used; if no options are provided, the current options for this action are used.

> Example:

```
cache_page "I'm the cached content", :controller => "lists",
  :action => "show"
```

`expire_page(options = {})`
> Expires the page that was cached with the options as a key.

> Example:

```
expire_page :controller => "lists", :action => "show"
```

Action caching

Action caching is similar to page caching in the fact that the entire output of the response is cached but different in that every request still goes through the ActionPack. The key benefit of this is that filters are run before the cache is served, which allows for authentication and other restrictions on whether someone is allowed to see the cache.

Example:

```
class ListsController < ApplicationController
  before_filter :authenticate, :except => :public
  caches_page   :public
```

```
  caches_action :show, :feed
end
```

In this example, the public action doesn't require authentication, so it's possible to use the faster page caching method. But both the show and feed actions are to be shielded behind the authenticate filter, so we need to implement those as action caches.

Action caching internally uses the fragment caching and an around filter to do the job. The fragment cache is named according to both the current host and the path. So a page that is accessed at *david.somewhere.com/lists/show/1* will result in a fragment named *david.somewhere.com/lists/show/1*. This allows the cacher to differentiate between *david.somewhere.com/lists/* and *jamis.somewhere.com/lists/*, which is a helpful way of assisting the subdomain-as-account-key pattern.

Fragment caching

Fragment caching is used for caching various blocks within templates without caching the entire action as a whole. This is useful when certain elements of an action change frequently or depend on a complicated state while other parts rarely change or can be shared among multiple parties. The caching is done using the cache helper available in the ActionView. A template with caching might look something like this:

```
<b>Hello <%= @name %></b>
<% cache do %>
  All the topics in the system:
  <%= render_collection_of_partials "topic", Topic.find_all %>
<% end %>
```

This cache will bind to the name of the action that called it. So, you could use `expire_fragment(:controller => "topics", :action => "list")` to invalidate it—if that was the controller/action used. This is not too helpful if you need to cache multiple fragments per action or if the action itself is cached using `caches_action`. Instead, we should qualify the name of the action used with something like this:

```
<% cache(:action => "list", :action_suffix => "all_topics") do %>
```

That would result in a name like */topics/list/all_topics*, which wouldn't conflict with any action cache or with another fragment using a different suffix. Note that the URL doesn't have to really exist or be callable. We're just using the `url_for` system to generate unique cache names that we can refer to later for expirations. The expiration call for this example would be `expire_fragment(:controller => "topics", :action => "list", :action_suffix => "all_topics")`.

Fragment stores. To use the fragment caching, you need to designate where the caches should be stored. This is done by assigning a fragment store, of which there are four different kinds:

FileStore
> Keeps the fragments on disk in the `cache_path`, works well for all types of environments, and shares the fragments for all the web server processes running off the same application directory.

MemoryStore
> Keeps the fragments in memory, which is fine for WEBrick and for FCGI (if you don't care that each FCGI process holds its own fragment store). It's not suitable for CGI as the process is thrown away at the end of each request. It can potentially also take up a lot of memory as each process keeps all the caches in memory.

DRbStore
> Keeps the fragments in the memory of a separate, shared DRb process. This works for all environments and keeps only one cache around for all processes, but it requires that you run and manage a separate DRb process.

MemCacheStore
> Works like DRbStore, but uses Danga's MemCache instead. Requires the ruby-memcache library: `gem install ruby-memcache`.

Configuration examples (*MemoryStore* is the default):

```
ActionController::Base.fragment_cache_store =
 :memory_store
```

```
ActionController::Base.fragment_cache_store =
 :file_store, "/path/to/cache/directory"
ActionController::Base.fragment_cache_store =
 :drb_store, "druby://localhost:9192"
ActionController::Base.fragment_cache_store =
 :mem_cache_store, "localhost"
ActionController::Base.fragment_cache_store =
 MyOwnStore.new("parameter")
```

Sweeping cache

Sweepers are the terminators of the caching world, responsible
for expiring caches when model objects change. They do this
by being half observers, half filters and implementing callbacks
for both roles. A sweeper example:

```
class ListSweeper < ActionController::Caching::Sweeper
  observe List, Item

  def after_save(record)
    list = record.is_a?(List) ? record : record.list
    expire_page(:controller => "lists", :action => %w( show public feed ),
     :id => list.id)
    expire_action(:controller => "lists", :action => "all")
    list.shares.each { |share| expire_page(:controller => "lists",
     :action => "show",
     :id => share.url_key) }
  end
end
```

The sweeper is assigned in the controllers that wish to have
their jobs performed using the cache_sweeper class method:

```
class ListsController < ApplicationController
  caches_action :index, :show, :public, :feed
  cache_sweeper :list_sweeper, :only => [ :edit, :destroy, :share ]
end
```

In the previous example, four actions are cached, and three
actions are responsible for expiring those caches.

Rails and Ajax

Ajax is an acronym for Asynchronous JavaScript and XML. A
primary characteristic of using Ajax is increased responsive-
ness and interactivity of webpages by allowing "behind the
scenes" interaction with the web server. This is intended to

increase the webpage's interactivity, speed, functionality, and usability.

Rails includes the Prototype JavaScript framework (see *http://www.prototypejs.org*) and the Scriptaculous JavaScript controls and visual effects library (*http://script.aculo.us*). If you wish to use these libraries and their helpers (`ActionView::Helpers::PrototypeHelper` and `ActionView::Helpers::ScriptaculousHelper`), you must do one of the following:

Use <%= `javascript_include_tag :defaults` %> in the HEAD section of your page (recommended)
> This function will return references to the JavaScript files created by the Rails command in your *public/javascripts* directory. Using it is recommended, as the browser can then cache the libraries instead of fetching all the functions anew on every request.

Use <%= `javascript_include_tag 'prototype'` %>
> As above, but will only include the Prototype core library, which means you are able to use all basic Ajax functionality. For the Scriptaculous-based JavaScript helpers, like visual effects, autocompletion, drag and drop, and so on, you should use the method described above.

Use <%= `define_javascript_functions` %>
> This will copy all the JavaScript support functions within a single script block. Not recommended.

JavaScriptHelper

Rails provides functionality for working with JavaScript in your views through helpers, such as the following:

`button_to_function(name, function, html_options = {})`
> Returns a link that will trigger a JavaScript `function` using the *onclick* handler.

> Examples:

```
button_to_function "Greeting", "alert('Hello world!')"
button_to_function "Delete",
                   "if confirm('Really?'){ do_delete(); }"
```

define_javascript_functions()

> Includes the ActionPack JavaScript libraries inside a single
> <script> tag. The function first includes *prototype.js* and
> then its core extensions, determined by filenames starting
> with prototype. Afterward, any additional scripts will be
> included in undefined order.

escape_javascript(javascript)

> Escapes carrier returns and single and double quotes for
> JavaScript segments.

javascript_tag(content)

> Returns a JavaScript tag with the content inside.

> Example:

```
javascript_tag "alert('All is good')"
# => <script type="text/javascript">
alert('All is good')</script>
```

link_to_function(name, function, html_options = {})

> Returns a link that will trigger a JavaScript function using
> the *onClick* handler and return *false* after the fact.

> Examples:

```
link_to_function "Greeting", "alert('Hello world!')"
link_to_function(image_tag("delete"),
"if confirm('Really?'){ do_delete(); }")
```

PrototypeHelper

PrototypeHelper provides a set of helpers for calling Prototype
JavaScript functions, including functionality to call remote
methods using Ajax. This means that you can call actions in
your controllers without reloading the page but still update
certain parts of it using injections into the DOM. The common-
use case is having a form that adds a new element to a list
without reloading the page.

The following is a list of helpers:

evaluate_remote_response()

> Returns eval(request.responseText), which is the Java-
> Script function that form_remote_tag can call

in :complete to evaluate a multiple-update return document using update_element_function calls.

form_remote_for(object_name, object, options = {}, &proc)
Alias for remote_form_for.

form_remote_tag(options = {})
Returns a form tag that will submit using XMLHttpRequest in the background instead of the regular reloading POST arrangement. Even though it's using JavaScript to serialize the form elements, the form submission will work just like a regular submission as viewed by the receiving side (all elements available in @params). The options for specifying the target with :url and defining callbacks is the same as link_to_remote.

A fall-through target for browsers that doesn't do JavaScript can be specified with the :action or :method options on :html.

Example:

```
form_remote_tag :html => { :action => url_for(:controller =>
  "some", :action => "place") }
```

The hash passed to the :html key is equivalent to the options (second) argument in the FormTagHelper.form_tag method.

By default the fall-through action is the same as the one specified in the :url (and the default method is :post).

link_to_remote(name, options = {}, html_options = {})
Returns a link to a remote action defined by options[:url] (using the url_for format) that's called in the background using XMLHttpRequest. The result of that request can then be inserted into a DOM object whose ID can be specified with options[:update]. Usually, the result would be a partial prepared by the controller with either render_partial or render_partial_collection.

Examples:

```
link_to_remote "Delete this post", :update => "posts",
  :url => { :action => "destroy", :id => post.id }
```

```
link_to_remote(image_tag("refresh"), :update => "emails",
    :url => { :action => "list_emails" })
```

You can also specify a hash for **options[:update]** to allow for easy redirection of output to another DOM element if a server-side error occurs.

Example:

```
link_to_remote "Delete this post",
    :url => { :action => "destroy", :id => post.id },
    :update => { :success => "posts", :failure => "error" }
```

Optionally, you can use the **options[:position]** parameter to influence how the target DOM element is updated. It must be one of **:before**, **:top**, **:bottom**, or **:after**.

By default, these remote requests are processed asynchronously during which time various JavaScript callbacks can be triggered (for progress indicators and the like). All callbacks get access to the request object, which holds the underlying XMLHttpRequest.

To access the server response, use **request.responseText**; to find out the HTTP status, use **request.status**.

Example:

```
link_to_remote word,
    :url => { :action => "undo", :n => word_counter },
    :complete => "undoRequestCompleted(request)"
```

The callbacks that may be specified are (in order):

:loading
> Called when the remote document is being loaded with data by the browser

:loaded
> Called when the browser has finished loading the remote document

:interactive
> Called when the user can interact with the remote document, even though it has not finished loading

:success
> Called when the XMLHttpRequest is completed, and the HTTP status code is in the 2XX range

`:failure`

>   Called when the XMLHttpRequest is completed, and the HTTP status code is not in the 2XX range

`:complete`

>   Called when the XMLHttpRequest is complete (fires after success/failure if they are present)

You can further refine `:success` and `:failure` by adding additional callbacks for specific status codes.

Example:

```
link_to_remote word,
    :url => { :action => "action" },
    404 => "alert('Not found...? Wrong URL...?')",
    :failure => "alert('HTTP Error ' + request.status + '!')"
```

A status code callback overrides the success/failure handlers, if present.

If for some reason or another, you need synchronous processing, which blocks the browser while the request is happening, specify `options[:type] = :synchronous`.

You can customize further browser-side call logic by passing code snippets in JavaScript via some optional parameters. In their order of use, these are:

`:confirm`

>   Adds confirmation dialog.

`:condition`

>   Performs remote request conditionally. Use this to describe browser-side conditions when a request should not be initiated.

`:before`

>   Called before a request is initiated.

`:after`

>   Called immediately after a request is initiated and before `:loading`.

`:submit`

>   Specifies the DOM element ID that's used as the parent of the form elements. By default, this is the

current form, but it could just as well be the ID of a table row or any other DOM element.

`observe_field(field_id, options = {})`

Observes the field with the DOM ID specified by `field_id` and makes an Ajax call when its contents have changed.

Required `options` are either of these two choices:

`:url`

url_for-style options for the action to call when the field has changed.

`:function`

Instead of making a remote call to a URL, you can specify a function to be called instead.

Additional options are:

`:frequency`

The frequency (in seconds) at which changes to this field will be detected. Not setting this option at all or setting it to a value equal to or less than zero will use event-based observation instead of time-based observation.

`:update`

Specifies the DOM ID of the element whose innerHTML should be updated with the XMLHttpRequest response text.

`:with`

A JavaScript expression specifying the parameters for the XMLHttpRequest. This defaults to value, which in the evaluated context refers to the new field value. If you specify a string without an equals sign (=), it will be extended to mean the form key to which the value should be assigned. So :with -> "term" gives 'term'=value". If a "=" is present, no extension will happen.

`:on`

Specifies which event handler to observe. By default, it's set to *changed* for text fields and areas and *click* for radio buttons and checkboxes. With this, you can specify it instead to be *blur* or *focus* or any other event.

Additionally, you may specify any of the options documented in `link_to_remote`.

`observe_form(form_id, options = {})`

Like `observe_field`, but operates on an entire form identified by the DOM ID `form_id`. `options` are the same as `observe_field`, except the default value of the `:with` option evaluates to the serialized (request string) value of the form.

`periodically_call_remote(options = {})`

Periodically calls the specified URL every x number of seconds, and updates the specified div with the results of the remote call. To specify the number of seconds, provide the option `:frequency` (default is 10). To specify the URL, provide the option `:url`. To specify a div by ID to update with the results, provide the option `:update` with the ID of the target div. For example:

```
<%= periodically_call_remote(:url => 'update',
                             :frequency => '20',
                             :update => 'my_target_div') %>
```

`remote_form_for(object_name, object, options = {}, &proc)`

Works like `form_remote_tag`, but uses `form_for` semantics. This method is also aliased as `form_remote_for`.

`remote_function(options)`

Returns the JavaScript needed for a remote function. Takes the same arguments as `link_to_remote`.

Example:

```
<select id="options" onchange="<%= remote_function (
    :update => "options",
    :url => { :action => :update_options }
  ) %>">
  <option value="0">Hello</option>
  <option value="1">World</option>
</select>
```

`submit_to_remote(name, value, options = {})`

Returns a button *input* tag that will submit form using XMLHttpRequest in the background instead of a regular

---

reloading POST arrangement. The options argument is the same as in `form_remote_tag`.

`update_element_function(element_id, options = {}, &block)`
Returns a JavaScript function (or expression) that'll update a DOM element according to the options passed:

:content

The content to use for updating. Can be left out if using block.

:action

Valid options are :update (assumed by default), :empty, and :remove.

:position

If the :action is :update, you can optionally specify one of the following: :before, :top, :bottom, and :after.

Examples:

```
<%= javascript_tag(update_element_function("products",
  :position => :bottom, :content => "<p>New product!</p>"))
%>

<% replacement_function = update_element_function("products")
do %>
  <p>Product 1</p>
  <p>Product 2</p>
<% end %>
<%= javascript_tag(replacement_function) %>
```

This method can also be used in combination with remote method call, where the result is evaluated afterward to cause multiple updates on a page.

Example:

```
# Calling view
<%= form_remote_tag :url => { :action => "buy" },
  :complete => evaluate_remote_response %>
all the inputs here...

# Controller action
def buy
  @product = Product.find(1)
end

# Returning view
```

```
<%= update_element_function(
    "cart", :action => :update, :position => :bottom,
    :content => "<p>New Product: #{@product.name}</p>")) %>
<% update_element_function("status", :binding => binding) do
%>
  You've bought a new product!
<% end %>
```

Notice how the second call doesn't need to be in an ERb
output block since it uses a block and passes in the binding
to render directly. However, this trick will only work in
ERb (not Builder or other template forms).

update_page(&block)

> Yields a JavaScriptGenerator and returns the generated
> JavaScript code. Use this to update multiple elements on
> a page in an Ajax response. See the section "JavaScript-
> Generator," earlier, for more information.

update_page_tag(&block)

> Works like update_page but wraps the generated Java-
> Script in a <script> tag. Use this to include generated
> JavaScript in an ERb template. See the earlier section
> "JavaScriptGenerator" for more information.

ScriptaculousHelper

The ScriptaculousHelper provides a set of helpers for calling
Scriptaculous JavaScript functions, including those that create
Ajax controls and visual effects.

The Scriptaculoushelpers' behavior can be tweaked with various options. See the documentation at *http://script.aculo.us* for
more information on using these helpers in your application.

The following is a list of helpers:

draggable_element(element_id, options = {})

> Makes the element with the DOM ID specified by
> element_id draggable.
>
> Example:
>
> ```
> <%= draggable_element("my_image", :revert => true)
> ```

`drop_receiving_element(element_id, options = {})`

Makes the element with the DOM ID specified by `element_id` receive dropped draggable elements (created by `draggable_element`) and make an Ajax call. By default, the called action gets the DOM ID of the element as parameter.

Example:

```
<%= drop_receiving_element("my_cart", :url =>
    { :controller => "cart", :action => "add" }) %>
```

`sortable_element(element_id, options = {})`

Makes the element with the DOM ID specified by `element_id` sortable by drag-and-drop, and makes an Ajax call whenever the sort order has changed. By default, the called action gets the serialized sortable element as parameter.

Example:

```
<%= sortable_element("my_list", :url =>
    { :action => "order" }) %>
```

`visual_effect(name, element_id = false, js_options = {})`

Returns a JavaScript snippet to be used on the Ajax callbacks for starting visual effects.

Example:

```
<%= link_to_remote "Reload", :update => "posts",
    :url => { :action => "reload" },
    :complete => visual_effect(:highlight, "posts",
    :duration => 0.5)
```

If no `element_id` is given, it assumes an *element*, which should be a local variable in the generated JavaScript execution context. This can be used, for example, with `drop_receiving_element`:

```
<%= drop_receiving_element (...), :loading ->
    visual_effect(:fade) %>
```

This would fade the element that was dropped on the drop receiving element.

Use `:toggle_appear`, `:toggle_slide`, and `:toggle_blind`—which will alternate between appear/fade, slidedown/

slideup, and blinddown/blindup, respectively—for tog-
gling visiual effects.

Real World Example: Honey-Do Task List

Just to get our feet wet in the Rails/Ajax world, let's create a
simple application that will manage our honey-do tasks. What
we want to achieve is to be able to dynamically add and remove
tasks, all using Scriptaculous and Prototype. Let's get started.

1. Create a new Rails application called "honey-do":

   ```
   rails honey-do
   ```

2. Now let's create the Task model with some fields:

   ```
   ./script/generate model Task name:string priority:integer
     completed:boolean
   ```

   Run the **rake** command to generate the database, then
   the command to run the migrations:

   ```
   rake db:create    # This is necessary only if the db isn't
                     # created and you are not using SQLite3
   rake db:migrate
   ```

3. Create the Tasks controller:

   ```
   ./script/generate controller tasks
   ```

4. Now that we have the infrastructure in place, let's start
   adding some code. First, let's add some methods to the
   Task model and give it a validator:

   ```ruby
   # app/models/task.rb

   class Task < ActiveRecord::Base

     validates_length_of :name, :minimum => 3,
                         :message =>
                           "must be at least 3 characters long"

     # This is our list of available priorities.
     def self.priorities
       %w(1 2 3 4 5)
     end

     # Helper method to get open tasks sorted by priority
     def self.open_tasks
       Task.find(:all, :order => [:priority], :conditions =>
       ["completed = ?", false])
   ```

```
      end

  end
```

Note that our Task model requires that the length of the name is at least three characters. We also created two static helper methods.

5. Now let's take a look at the controller:

```
# app/controllers/tasks_controller.rb

class TasksController < ApplicationController

  def index
    @tasks = Task.open_tasks
  end

  # This action is only called via Ajax and renders
  # the results to the
  # 'app/views/tasks/_task_list.html.erb' partial
  def create
    task = Task.new(params[:task])
    unless task.save
      flash[:error] = "Unable to add task"
    end
    @tasks = Task.open_tasks
    render :partial => "task_list", :layout => false
  end

  # This action is only called via Ajax and renders
  # the results to the
  #'app/views/tasks/_task_list.html.erb' partial
  def complete
    task = Task.find(params[:id])
    task.completed = true
    unless task.save
      flash[:error] = "Unable to mark task as completed"
    end
    @tasks = Task.open_tasks
    render :partial => "task_list", :layout -> false
  end

end
```

In our controller, we have three actions. The first is **index**, which loads the @tasks variable with the results of Task.open_tasks. This code calls the method open_tasks statically from within the Task model.

The next two actions are similar in that they both are only called via Ajax requests. The first, **create**, will create a task from the request parameters and then render the partial **task_list**, which we will get to. The **complete** action marks the task as complete, then renders the **task_list** partial.

6. Now we need a view:

```erb
# app/views/tasks/index.html.erb

<h1>My Tasks</h1>

<!-- Partial include which contains our task list -->
<div id="task_list">
  <%= render :partial => "task_list", :locals =>
    { :tasks => @tasks } %>
</div>

<!-- Javascript / scriptaculous call to show form -->
<a href="#" onclick="$('task_name').clear();
    <!-- Clear the form first -->
                      Effect.BlindDown('task_form');
                      return false;">Add Task</a>

<!-- Here is our 'add task' form.  It is hidden by default
--> <div id="task_form" style="display: none;">

<!-- Using the form_remote_tag which builds the
  AJAX code for us -->
  <% form_remote_tag :url => { :action => "create" },
                      :update => "task_list",
                      :complete => visual_effect(:fade,
                      "task_form") do %>

    <p>
      <%= label(:task, :name) %>
      <%= text_field :task, :name, :size => 38 %>
    </p>

    <p>
      <%= label(:task, :priority) %>
      <%= select(:task, :priority, Task.priorities) %>
    </p>

    <%= submit_tag "Add Task", :class => "submit" %>

<!-- One more scriptaculous effect to hide the form -->
    <%= button_to_function "Nevermind",
                            visual_effect(:fade,
                            "task_form"),
                            :class => "submit" %>

  <% end %>
```

```
    </div>
```

In our view, we have four main sections. The first is our
h1 tag, which just shows the header. Second, we have
our partial include, which renders the partial **task_list**
and provides it the **@tasks** object.

Third is a link to display the form, which uses the Scriptaculous effects library. Note that in the onclick is
$('task_name').clear; this is Prototype code, which
finds the **dom** element by the **id task_name** and clears the
value. (For more information on how to use Prototype
functionality, go to *http://www.prototypejs.org*.)

Fourth, we have our form which is generated with a
form_remote_tag. As you can see, the **form_remote_tag**
specifies that the form is to be submitted via Ajax to the
action **update**, and when it is complete, the **fade** visual
effect should happen on the DOM element with ID of
task_form.

We also added a Nevermind button, which performs the
same fade as the submit does without actually submit-
ting the form.

7. Now let's look at our partial:

```
<ul>
<% @tasks.each do |task| %>
  <li>
    <table width="100%">
      <tr>
        <td align="left">
          <%= task.priority %> - <%= task.name %>
        </td>
        <td align="right">
          <%= link_to_remote "Mark as Complete",
            :url => { :action => "complete", :id => task },
            .update )"task_list" %>
        </td>
      </tr>
    </table>
  </li>
<% end %>
</ul>
```

The partial we included is an unordered list (ul) with a table inside each of the list items (li). The table provides easy left and right alignment for the contents and the link.

We are using the helper link_to_remote to allow the user to mark the task as completed by clicking on the link. What it will do is call the remote action complete and then rerender the task_list DOM element from the results.

8. Add a touch of style to the application by creating a stylesheet:

```
/* public/stylesheets/application.css */

body {
  font-family: Arial, Helvetica, sans-serif; }

#task_list {
  background-color: #efefef;
  width: 500px;
  padding: 10px;
  margin-bottom: 10px; }

#task_list ul {
  margin: 0;
  padding: 0;
  list-style: none; }

#task_form {
  display: block;
  border: 1px dashed #ccc;
  background-color: #E6E6B6;
  width: 500px;
  padding: 10px;
  margin-top: 10px; }

#task_form p {
  margin: 5px 0;
  padding: 0; }

#task_form label {
  float: left;
  width: 70px;
  font-size: 1.1em;
  text-align: right;
  padding-right: 10px; }

input[type=submit], input[type=button], input[type=text],
select {
```

```
    font-size: 1.1em;
    font-weight: bold;
    padding: 2px 4px;
    min-width: 50px; }

#task_form input.submit {
    margin: 10px 0 0 80px;
    color: #000; }
```

9. Create a layout to include the stylesheet and JavaScript files needed:

```
# ap/views/layouts/application.html.erb

<html>
  <head>
    <title>Honey-Do Task List</title>
    <%= javascript_include_tag :defaults %>
    <%- stylesheet_link_tag "application" %>
  </head>
  <body>

    <%= yield %>

  </body>
</html>
```

We are using two helpers—javascript_include_tag and stylesheet_link_tag—in the layout.

10. We're about there. Let's just remove the default *in dex.html* file in the public folder:

```
rm public/index.html
```

and then update our *config/routes.rb* file:

```
ActionController::Routing::Routes.draw do |map|
    map.root :controller -> "tasks"
    map.connect ':controller/:action/:id'
    map.connect ':controller/:action/:id.:format'
end
```

11. That should be it. Let's start the web server and test it out. Your browser should look similar to the one in Figure 1-4.

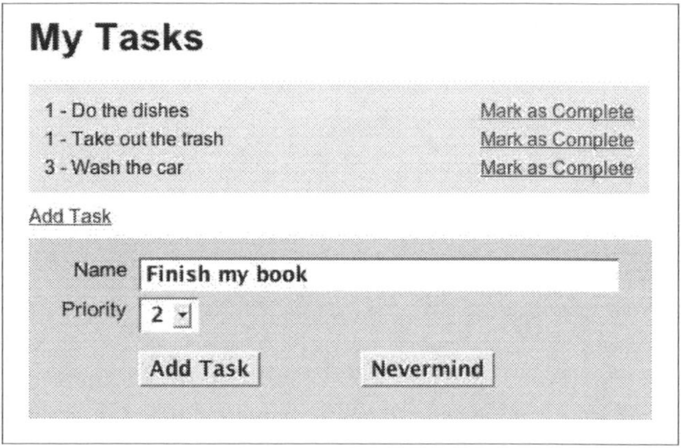

My Tasks

1 - Do the dishes	Mark as Complete
1 - Take out the trash	Mark as Complete
3 - Wash the car	Mark as Complete

Add Task

Name **Finish my book**
Priority 2

Add Task   **Nevermind**

Figure 1-4. Honey-do task list screenshot

Routing

The routing module provides URL rewriting in native Ruby. It's a way to redirect incoming requests to controllers and actions. This replaces *mod_rewrite* rules. Best of all, Rails's Routing works with any web server. Routes are defined in *routes.rb* in your *RAILS_ROOT/config* directory.

Routing Basics

Consider the following route, installed by Rails when you generate your application:

```
map.connect ':controller/:action/:id'
```

This route states that it expects requests to consist of a :controller followed by an :action that in turn is fed some :id.

Suppose you get an incoming request for */blog/edit/22*. You'll end up with:

```
params = { :controller => 'blog',
           :action     => 'edit',
           :id         => '22'    }
```

Think of creating routes as drawing a map for your requests. The map tells them where to go based on some predefined pattern:

```
ActionController::Routing::Routes.draw do |map|
  Pattern 1 tells some request to go to one place
  Pattern 2 tell them to go to another
  ...
end
```

The following symbols are special:

`:controller`

> Maps to your controller name

`:action`

> Maps to an action with your controllers

Other names simply map to a parameter, as in the case of `:id`.

Route priority

Routes are prioritized from top to bottom. The last route in that file is the lowest priority and will be applied last. If no route matches, 404 is returned.

Within blocks, the empty pattern is the highest priority. In practice, this works out nicely:

```
ActionController::Routing::Routes.draw do |map|
  map.with_options :controller => 'blog' do |blog|
    blog.show '',  :action => 'list'
  end
  map.connect ':controller/:action/:view'
end
```

In this case, invoking blog controller (with a URL like */blog/*) without parameters will activate the `list` action by default.

Default routes and default parameters

Setting a default route is straightforward in Rails—you simply append a hash at the end of your mapping to set any default parameters. For example:

```
ActionController::Routing:Routes.draw do |map|
  map.connect ':controller/:action/:id', :controller => 'blog'
end
```

This sets up the blog as the default controller if no other is specified. This means a visiting / would invoke the blog controller.

More formally, you can define defaults in a route with the :defaults key:

```
map.connect ':controller/:action/:id', :action => 'show', :defaults =>
  { :page => 'Dashboard' }
```

Named routes

Routes can be named with the syntax map.name_of_route options, allowing for easy reference within your source as name_of_route_url for the full URL and name_of_route_path for the URI path. For example:

```
# In routes.rb
map.login 'login', :controller => 'accounts', :action => 'login'

# With render, redirect_to, tests, etc.
redirect_to login_url
```

Arguments can be passed as well:

```
redirect_to show_item_path(:id => 25)
```

Use map.root as a shorthand to name a route for the root path:

```
# In routes.rb
map.root :controller => 'blogs'

# would recognize http://www.example.com/ as
# params = { :controller => 'blogs', :action => 'index' }

# and provide these named routes
root_url   # => 'http://www.example.com/'
root_path  # => ''

# In routes.rb
map.with_options :controller => 'blog' do |blog|
  blog.show   '',             :action => 'list'
  blog.delete 'delete/:id',   :action => 'delete',
  blog.edit   'edit/:id',     :action => 'edit'
end

# provides named routes for show, delete, and edit
link_to @article.title, show_path(:id => @article.id)
```

When using `with_options`, the route is simply named after the method you call on the block parameter rather than map.

Pretty URLs

Routes can generate pretty URLs. For example:

```
map.connect 'articles/:year/:month/:day',
            :controller => 'articles',
            :action     => 'find_by_date',
            :year       => /\d{4}/,
            :month      => /\d{1,2}/,
            :day        => /\d{1,2}/

# Using the route above, the url below maps to:
# params = {:year => '2008', :month => '11', :day => '06'}
# http://localhost:3000/articles/2008/11/06
```

Regular expressions and parameters

You can specify a regular expression to define a format for a parameter:

```
map.geocode 'geocode/:postalcode', :controller => 'geocode',
            :action => 'show', :postalcode => /\d{5}(-\d{4})?/
```

Or more formally:

```
map.geocode 'geocode/:postalcode', :controller => 'geocode',
            :action => 'show', :requirements =>
            { :postalcode => /\d{5}(-\d{4})?/ }
```

Route globbing

Specifying *[string] as part of a rule like:

```
map.connect '*path' , :controller => 'blog' , :action => 'unrecognized?'
```

will glob all remaining parts of the route that were not recognized earlier. This idiom must appear at the end of the path. The globbed values are in `params[:path]` in this case.

Route conditions

With conditions, you can define restrictions on routes. Currently the only valid condition is `:method:`, which allows you to specify which method can access the route. Possible values are `:post`, `:get`, `:put`, `:delete`, and `:any`. The default value is `:any`, which means that any method can access the route.

Example:

```
map.connect 'post/:id', :controller => 'posts',
            :action => 'show',
            :conditions => { :method => :get }
map.connect 'post/:id', :controller => 'posts', :action =>
            'create_comment',
            :conditions => { :method => :post }
```

Now, if you POST to `/posts/:id`, it will route to the `create_comment` action. A GET on the same URL will route to the show action.

Reloading routes

If you need to reload your routes, you can use:

```
ActionController::Routing::Routes.reload
```

This will clear all named routes and reload *routes.rb* if the file has been modified from the last load. You can also use the ERb command **reload!** to force reloading.

REST

In Rails 2.1, one of the largest improvements made to the Rails framework was the addition of RESTful resources through `ActionController::Resources`. A RESTful resource is something that can be pointed at and will respond with a representation of the data requested. Instead of assigning the action to be taken within the parameters of the request or in the path, the method used along with the path determines what will happen.

For example, let's take a product model and make it RESTful. To do this, we need to add the line into *routes.rb*:

```
map.resources :products
```

By adding this line into the routes configuration, the Product model is now a RESTful resource.

Our routes now might look something like Table 1-3.

Table 1-3. RESTful routes

Method	Path	Action	Helper
GET	/products	index	products_url
GET	/products/new	new	new_product_url
POST	/products	create	products_ur
GET	/products/1/edit	edit	edit_product_url(:id => 1)
PUT	/products/1	update	products_url(:id => 1)
GET	/products/1	show	product_url(:id => 1)
DELETE	/products/1	destroy	product_url(:id => 1)

As you can see, the combination of the request method used and the URL will determine the action.

RESTful Resources

There are three different ways to add resources to your routes:

Simple
　　Allows resource to be accessed RESTfully:

```
map.resources :products, :users
```

Nested
　　Allows resources to be accessed RESTfully within a container controller:

```
map.resources :admin do |admin|
  admin.resources :users
end
```

Customized
　　Resources that have customized options. Available options are:

:collection

Adds named routes for other actions that operate on the collection. Takes a hash of `#{action}` => `#{method}`; method is `:get/:post/:put/:delete`, or `:any` if the method does not matter. These routes map to a URL like `/messages/rss`, with a route of `rss_messages_url`.

Example:

```
map.resources :products,
              :collection => { :sort => :put }
```

:member

Same as `:collection` but for actions that operate on a specific member.

Example:

```
map.resources :products,
              :member => { :out_of_stock => :delete }
```

:new

Same as `:collection` but for actions that operate on the new resource action.

Example:

```
map.resources :products,
              :new => { :preview => :post }
```

:controller

Specifes the controller name for the routes.

Example:

```
map.resources :products,
              :controller => 'products'
```

:singular

Specifies the singular name used in the member routes.

Example:

```
map.resources :products,
              :singular => 'product'
```

:requirements

Sets custom routing parameter requirements.

Example:

```
map.resources :products,
              :controller => 'products',
              :action => 'create',
              :requirements => { :name => /\d{3}?/ }
```

:conditions

Specifies custom routing recognition conditions. Resources set the :method value for the method-specific
routes.

Example:

```
map.resources :products,
              :controller => 'products',
              :action => 'show',
              :conditions => { :method => :get }
```

:path_prefix

Sets a prefix to the routes with required route
variables.

Example:

```
map.resources :products
map.resources :product_reviews, :path_prefix =>
  '/reviews/:product_id'
```

:name_prefix

Override the generic named routes in a nested
resource.

Example:

```
map.resources :products, :name_prefix => 'item_'
```

Sample RESTful Rails Application

Let's create a simple Rails application that will demonstrate
some of the useful features of REST. The following example
assumes that you are using Rails 2.1.0 or later:

1. Create a new Rails application:

   ```
   rails my_restful_app
   ```

2. In your new application, add the User model using Rails
   scaffolding:

```
./script/generate scaffold User first_name:string /
  last_name:string phone:string
```

Once you run this, a handful of new files are generated,
including a migration script. Run the migration script:

```
rake db:migrate
```

Take a look at the files that were generated and modified. First,
look at *config/routes.rb*:

```
ActionController::Routing::Routes.draw do |map|
  ...
  map.resources :users
  ...
end
```

The code **map.resources :users** was added, indicating that the
application is to treat the User model as a RESTful resource.

Now let's take a look at the generated controller:

```
class UsersController < ApplicationController
  # GET /users
  # GET /users.xml
  def index
    @users = User.find(:all)

    respond_to do |format|
      format.html # index.html.erb
      format.xml  { render :xml => @users }
    end
  end

  # GET /users/1
  # GET /users/1.xml
  def show
    @user = User.find(params[:id])

    respond_to do |format|
      format.html # show.html.erb
      format.xml  { render :xml => @user }
    end
  end

  # GET /users/new
  # GET /users/new.xml
  def new
    @user = User.new

    respond_to do |format|
      format.html # new.html.erb
      format.xml  { render :xml => @user }
```

```
    end
  end

# GET /users/1/edit
def edit
  @user = User.find(params[:id])
end

# POST /users
# POST /users.xml
def create
  @user = User.new(params[:user])

  respond_to do |format|
    if @user.save
      flash[:notice] = 'User was successfully created.'
      format.html { redirect_to(@user) }
      format.xml  { render :xml => @user, :status =>
        :created, :location => @user }
    else
      format.html { render :action => "new" }
      format.xml  { render :xml => @user.errors, :status =>
        :unprocessable_entity }
    end
  end
end

# PUT /users/1
# PUT /users/1.xml
def update
  @user = User.find(params[:id])

  respond_to do |format|
    if @user.update_attributes(params[:user])
      flash[:notice] = 'User was successfully updated.'
      format.html { redirect_to(@user) }
      format.xml  { head :ok }
    else
      format.html { render :action => "edit" }
      format.xml  { render :xml => @user.errors, :status =>
        :unprocessable_entity }
    end
  end
end

# DELETE /users/1
# DELETE /users/1.xml
def destroy
  @user = User.find(params[:id])
  @user.destroy

  respond_to do |format|
    format.html { redirect_to(users_url) }
    format.xml  { head :ok }
```

```
      end
    end
  end
```

The controller has an action for all seven RESTful actions. Above each action is a URL that invokes that action.

Each action in this controller also contains a respond_to block. This determines the format of the response based on the request URL. For example, if you were to go point your browser to *http://localhost:3000/users*, it would return the HTML view for the index action. If you were to append *.xml* to the end of the URL, making it *http://localhost:3000/users.xml*, the action would recognize the difference and return the response in XML format.

ActionMailer

ActionMailer is used for sending emails within your Rails application.

To create an ActionMailer model, you can use the generator script:

```
./script/generate mailer Mailer
```

```
    create  app/views/mailer
    create  app/models/mailer.rb
```

When the script is run, the model *app/models/mailer.rb* and the folder *app/views/mailer* are created. Emails are defined by creating methods within the mailer model that are used to pass variables to the email template, modify options, and add attachments.

Example:

```
class Mailer < ActionMailer::Base

  def welcome_email(user)
    recipients user.email
    from       "noreply@solidcoresolutions.com"
    subject    "Welcome to Solid Core Solutions"
    body       :user => user
  end
```

```
end
```

The available configuration options are:

`:recipients`

> Takes one or more email addresses. These addresses are where your email will be delivered. Sets the *To:* header.

`:subject`

> The subject of your email. Sets the *Subject:* header.

`:from`

> Who the email you are sending is from. Sets the *From:* header.

`:cc`

> Takes one or more email addresses. These addresses will receive a carbon copy of your email. Sets the *Cc:* header.

`:bcc`

> Takes one or more email addresses. These addresses will receive a blind carbon copy of your email. Sets the *Bcc:* header.

`:sent_on`

> The date on which the message was sent. If not set, the header will be set by the delivery agent.

`:content_type`

> Specifies the content type of the message (defaults to `text/plain`).

`:headers`

> Specifies additional headers to be set for the message, e.g., headers *X-Mail-Count => 107370*.

Every mailer class has a corresponding view directory, which contains email templates. The templates are `.html.erb` files with the same name as the method calling them. For example, to send the *welcome_email* in the mailer class shown earlier, a template with the filename *welcome_email.html.erb* needs to be in the *app/views/mailer*.

Emails are sent as plain text by default. An example of a plain text email view might look like this:

```
Welcome <%= user.first_name %>,
Thank you for registering. Please visit us again.
```

Sending an Email

To send an email using ActiveMailer, you can use the **deliver** method:

```
Mailer.deliver_welcome_email(eric) # Sends the welcome_email
```

You can also create the mail as an object, then deliver it:

```
email = Mailer.deliver_welcome_email(eric)
Mailer.deliver(email)
```

HTML and Multipart Emails

To send an HTML email, make sure your view contains HTML and the **content_type** is set to **text/html**:

```
class Mailer < ActionMailer::Base

  def newsletter(user)
    recipients user.email
    from       "noreply@solidcoresolutions.com"
    subject    "Solid Core Solutions Newsletter"
    body       :user => user
    content_type "text/html"
  end

end
```

Sending a multipart email is similar to sending an HTML email. For example, to send both a plain text and HTML version of a newsletter, your code could look like this:

```
class Mailer < ActionMailer::Base

  def newsletter(user)
    recipients user.email
    from       "noreply@solidcoresolutions.com"
    subject    "Solid Core Solutions Newsletter"

    part :content_type => "text/html",
        :body => render_message("newsletter.text.html.erb",
        :user => user)

    part "text/plain" do |p|
      p.body = render_message("newsletter.text.plain.erb",
        :user => user)
```

```
      p.transfer_encoding = "base64"
    end

  end

end
```

For the previous example to work, you will also need the *app/
views/mailer/newsletter.text.html.erb*   and   *app/views/mailer/
newsletter.text.plain.erb* views to exist.

Attachments

It is fairly simple to add attachments to your emails. You can
add them using the **attachment** method. For example:

```
class Mailer < ActionMailer::Base

  def newsletter(user)
    recipients user.email
    from       "noreply@solidcoresolutions.com"
    subject    "Solid Core Solutions Newsletter"
    body       :user => user

    attachment :content_type => "image/jpeg",
               :body => File.read("/path/to/image.jpg")

  end

end
```

Action Web Services

Rails allows for rapid development of web services. Web services can be broken down into two main parts: servers and clients. Servers provide the service that is being accessed, and the
clients are the applications that access them. Most web services
are based on one of three architectures: REST, XML-RPC, or
SOAP.

What Can You Do with Web Services Under Rails?

There are many web services available for you to use, from
Yahoo! Search to Flickr to everything in between. Visit *http://*

www.programmableweb.com/apis for hundreds of useful web
service providers. For additional information on web services
using Rails, I suggest reading Kevin Marshall's *Short Cut: Web
Services on Rails* at *http://www.oreilly.com/catalog/
9780596527969*.

Using REST

REST is often referred to as the simplest web service architecture. For the most part, REST is operations work just like
standard webpage requests. The main advantages of using
REST over XML-RPC or SOAP are:

- It is lightweight—not a lot of extra XML markup
- It produces human-readable results
- It is easy to build—no toolkits required

REST is rapidly becoming the web service framework of choice
and is now being used by all of Yahoo!'s web services, including
Flickr. del.icio.us API, bloglines, technorati, eBay, and Ama-
zon use it as well.

The following is a step-by-step example of how to use Yahoo!
Search REST API. For this example to work, you will need an
application ID. Register at *http://api.search.yahoo.com/webser
vices/register_application* and you will get one.

1. Create a new Rails application:

    ```
    rails myapp
    ```

2. In the new Rails application folder, create a controller to
   access web services:

    ```
    ./script/generate controller web_services
    ```

3. Create an action in the controller that will call the
   Yahoo! Search REST API:

    ```
    class WebServicesController < ApplicationController
      def yahoo_search
        query = CGI.escape("Web Services on Rails")
        appid = "YOUR YAHOO APPLICATION ID"
        url = "http://search.yahooapis.com" +
            "/WebSearchService/V1/webSearch?" +
    ```

```
            "appid=#{yahookey}&query=#{query}" +
            "&results=3&start=1"
  puts url
  result = Net::HTTP.get(URI(url))
  @doc = REXML::Document.new result
end
end
```

4. Now create a view to display the search results. It would be *app/views/web_services/yahoo_search.html.erb* here:

```
<% @doc.root.each_element do |res| %>
  <b>Title:</b> <%= res[0].text.to_s %><br/>
  <b>Summary:</b> <%= res[1].text.to_s %><br/>
  <b>Link:</b> <%= link_to res[2].text.to_s,
    res[2].text.to_s %><br/><br/>
<% end %>
```

5. Start your web server and go to *http://localhost:3000/web_services/yahoo_search* in your browser. Your results should look similar to this:

```
Title: O'Reilly Media | Web Services on Rails
Summary: "Web Services on Rails by Kevin Marshall ...
Link: http://www.oreilly.com/catalog/9780596527969/

Title: ActionWebService: Web services on Rails |
Summary: About "ActionWebService: Web services on Rails" ...
Link: http://manuals.rubyonrails.com/read/book/10

Title: Crossing borders: REST on Rails
Summary: ... borders series introduced Ruby on Rails as an ...
Link: http://www-128.ibm.com/developerworks/java/...
```

Using XML-RPC

XML-RPC is easier to use than SOAP, which makes it much simpler to understand, implement, and debug. To demonstrate how to create a web service client using XML-RPC, let's create a small application that will display photos from Flickr (*http://www.flickr.com*). In this example, we will use the same application that we created previously for accessing Yahoo! Search via REST:

1. Go to *http://www.flickr.com/services/api/keys/apply* to get a Flickr API.

2. Add a new action to *web_services_controller.rb*:

```
require 'xmlrpc/client' # This is required to access
XMLRPC::Client

class WebServicesController < ApplicationController

  ...

  def flickr
    flickruri = "http://www.flickr.com/services/xmlrpc/"
    server = XMLRPC::Client.new2(flickruri)
    flickrkey = "YOUR FLICKR SERVICES API KEY"
    details = { :api_key => flickrkey, :per_page => "10",
                :tags => "summer, beach, fun" }
    result = server.call("flickr.photos.search", details)
    @doc = REXML::Document.new result
  end

end
```

3. Now create a view to display the image results. The view should be *app/views/web_services/flickr.html.erb*:

```
<% @doc.root.each_element do |res|
  image_url = "http://static.flickr.com/" +
              "#{res.attributes["server"]}/" +
              "#{res.attributes["id"]}_" +
              "#{res.attributes["secret"]}.jpg"
%>
<%= image_tag(image_url, :border => "0",
    :height => "100") %><br/>
<%= res.attributes["title"] %>
<br/><br/>
<% end %>
```

4. Start your web server and go to *http://localhost:3000/web_services/flickr* in your browser.

Using SOAP

SOAP is probably the most widely used web services framework right now. Some advantages of SOAP are:

• It is easy to use (well, sometimes)

• It is strict—type checking, adheres to a contract

• It has wide availability of development tools and example code

Let's add one more web services client to our application created in the last two sections. This time, we're going to use

SOAP to access the longitude and latitude of an address, then use the Google Map API to display the map in the view. Here we go:

1. Add a new action to our *web_services_controller.rb*:

```ruby
...
require 'soap/wsdlDriver'

class WebServicesController < ApplicationController

  ...

  def geocoder_lookup
    address = "1005 Gravenstein Highway North " +
              "Sebastopol, CA 95472"
    wsdl = "http://geocoder.us/dist/eg/clients/" +
           "GeoCoderPHP.wsdl"
    driver = SOAP::WSDLDriverFactory.new(wsdl).
             create_rpc_driver
    @results = driver.geocode(address)
  end

end
```

In this step, we created the action *geocoder_lookup* and are using the geocoder.us web API to get the latitude and longitude of the address we provide.

As you can see, we are using the `SOAP::WSDLDriverFac tory` to generate a SOAP driver from the WSDL URL. A WSDL, or Web Services Description Language, is an XML format for describing network services as a set of endpoints operating on messages containing either document- or procedure-oriented information. It defines what can be done using the API.

Next, we call the method *geocode* from the driver. This is a method defined within the WSDL file, and it returns an array of address-related information. We pass it to the view.

2. Next, create a view to display the map. The view would be *app/views/web_services/geocode_lookup.html.erb*:

```html
<script type="text/javascript"
        src="http://www.google.com/jsapi?key=
             YOUR_GOOGLE_MAPS_API_KEY"></script>
<script type="text/javascript">
```

```
google.load("maps", "2.x");

// Call this function when the page has been loaded
function initialize() {
    var map = new google.maps.Map2(document.
            getElementById("map"));
    map.setCenter(new google.maps.
            LatLng(<%= @results.first.lat %>,
            <%= @results.first.long %>), 13);
}

google.setOnLoadCallback(initialize);
</script>

<div id="map" style="width: 500px; height: 300px"></div>
```

The code in our view is a basic Google API call via their JavaScript library, which renders the map to the **div** with **id="map"**.

3. Start your web server and go to *http://localhost:3000/web _services/geocode_lookup* in your browser.

Logging

The **logger** class provides a simple but sophisticated logging utility that anyone can use because it's included in the Ruby 1.8.x standard library. This class can generally be accessed from anywhere inside your Ruby code and is an excellent tool for debugging your application.

Rails automatically generates a logfile that corresponds to your environment in the **log** folder.

To log a message from a controller or model, access the Rails logger instance with the **logger** method:

```
class ProductController < ActionController::Base
  def index
    logger.info 'This is my message'
  end
end
```

From outside a controller or model, you can either pass the **logger** instance or access it with the constant **RAILS_DEFAULT_LOGGER**.

The messages will have varying levels (info, error, etc.), reflecting their varying importance. The levels, and their meanings, are:

FATAL
: An unhandleable error that results in a program crash

ERROR
: A handleable error condition

WARN
: A warning

INFO
: Generic (useful) information about system operation

DEBUG
: Low-level information for developers

So each message has a level, and the Logger itself has a level, which acts as a filter, so you can control the amount of information emitted from the logger without having to remove actual messages.

For instance, in a production system, you may have your logger(s) set to INFO (or WARN if you don't want the logfiles growing large with repetitive information). When you are developing it, though, you probably want to know about the program's internal state and thus set them to DEBUG.

Example.

```
logger.debug("Created logger")
logger.info("Program started")
logger.warn("Nothing to do!")

begin
  File.each_line(path) do |line|
    unless line =~ /^(\w+) = (.*)$/
      log.error("Line in wrong format. #{line}")
    end
  end
rescue => err
  logger.fatal("Caught exception; exiting")
  logger.fatal(err)
end
```

Because the Logger's level is set to WARN, only the warning, error, and fatal messages are recorded. The debug and info messages are silently discarded.

Filtering Sensitive Parameters

When Rails receives a request, ActionController logs the request parameters. This is very handy for debugging, but sometimes we would rather hide parameters like passwords from the logs. This is possible with the filter_parameter_logging class:

```
class ApplicationController < ActionController::Base
  filter_parameter_logging :password
end
```

This will cause any parameter name matching password to have its value replaced with [FILTERED] in the log. To filter multiple parameters, simply add them as extra arguments to filter_parameter_logging by separating them with commas.

Creating Additional Loggers

Sometimes instead of logging to a default Rails log, we may want to write to a separate log, which could be emailed or downloaded.

To do this, we would need to create a new class that would extend the logger:

```
# lib/archive_logger.rb

class ArchiveLogger < Logger
  def format_message(severity, timestamp, progname, msg)
    "#{timestamp.to_formatted_s(:db)} #{severity} #{msg}\n"
  end
end
```

To use the new ArchiveLogger, instantiate it with a File instance:

```
logfile = File.open('/path/to/audit.log', 'a')
archive_log = ArchiveLogger.new(logfile)
```

Your new log is now ready to use by calling methods on it, like `archive_log.info` message.

One important point to remember is that the `logfile` object does not implicitly flush to the file by default. This means that your code must call `logfile.flush` for the data to be written out. Alternatively, you can set `logfile.sync = true` to turn on implicit flushing.

Logging on the Console

When using the console, you may not see all the logs that would normally be added to the Rails log. To enable logging on the console, type:

```
ActiveRecord::Base.logger = Logger.new(STDOUT)
```

For more information on how to use the Logger, visit Ryan Bates's Railscast about it at *http://railscasts.com/episodes/56* or Mike Naberezny's blog article at *http://maintainable.com/articles/rails_logging_tips*.

ActiveResource

ActiveResource lets you declare and consume web services using an ActiveRecord-like interface. It can also be used to communicate between two Rails applications. For ActiveResource to work, the web service must:

- Understand RESTful URLs
- Respond to requests with a single XML-serialized object
- Make appropriate use of HTTP status codes (404 if the requested record cannot be found, 422 if any validations fail, etc.)

As an example, let's create a simple Rails app that manages DVD collections and another that accesses it via ActiveResource:

1. Create a Rails application named *my_video_library*:

```
rails my_video_library
```

2. In your new Rails app, create a scaffold for *dvd*:

```
./script/generate scaffold dvd title:string rating:string \
    description:string
```

3. Run the migration scripts:

```
rake db:migrate
```

4. Run the server on port 3000:

```
./script/server -p 3000
```

Now you can test the application by going to *http://lo calhost:3000/dvds* in your browser. Go ahead and add some DVDs so we can access them using the other app.

Now that we have our first app up and running, let's create the second Rails app to access the first:

1. Create a new Rails application named *another_library*:

```
rails another_library
```

2. Now create a controller named *my_dvds*:

```
./script/generate controller my_dvds
```

3. Create a class that represents the DVD using ActiveResource in *lib/dvd.rb*:

```
class Dvd < ActiveResource::Base
  self.site = "http://localhost:3000"

  # get all dvds
  def self.all
    Dvd.find(:all)
  end
end
```

4. We're all set up now. Let's get the list of DVDs with *my_dvds_controller.rb*:

```
class MyDvdsController < ApplicationController
  def index
    @dvds = Dvd.all
  end
end
```

with the view *app/views/index.html.erb*:

```
<% @dvds.each do |dvd| %>
  <%= dvd.title %><br/>
```

```
    <%= dvd.rating %><br/>
    <%= dvd.description %><br/><br/>
  <% end %>
```

5. Start up the new server on port 3001:

    ```
    ./script/server -p 3001
    ```

6. Open another web browser and go to *http://localhost: 3001/my_dvds*. If you added DVDs in the other app, you should see them here.

Plugins

Rails plugins are extensions or modifications to the core Rails framework. Using plugins allows developers to share code without affecting the stable code base.

To see a list of plugin repositories, you can use:

```
./script/plugin discover
```

To add a plugin repository by URL, type:

```
./script/plugin source [url]
```

To remove plugin repositories, type:

```
./script/plugin unsource [url]
```

To install a plugin into your Rails app, type:

```
./script/plugin install [name of plugin, or the url to the desired plugin]
```

To generate documentation on your plugins, you can use:

```
rake rdoc:plugins
```

This will create HTML documentation files in *doc/plugins*.

To find out more about plugins, including available plugins that can be installed into your Rails apps, go to:

*   *http://agilewebdevelopment.com/plugins*
*   *http://wiki.rubyonrails.org/rails/pages/Plugins*

Capistrano

Capistrano is a standalone utility that is used for automating tasks via SSH on remote servers. It was originally created by Jamis Buck (*http://jamisbuck.org*) and developed to help manage application deployment processes.

Capistrano uses tasks, similar to Rake. These tasks can include commands that are executed on servers. In addition, you can define roles for your servers and designate certain tasks to specific roles.

One of the common misunderstandings of Capistrano is where it needs to be installed. Because Capistrano runs commands via SSH, it needs to be installed only on the machines from which the server is being deployed.

Capistrano is a gem and can be installed by running:

```
sudo gem install capistrano
```

Two files are required to use Capistrano in a Rails application. You can generate these files by using the **capify** script. For example, if you are already in the Rails root folder:

```
$ capify .
[add] writing `./Capfile'
[add] writing `./config/deploy.rb'
[done] capified!
```

To view the available tasks, type:

```
cap -T
```

To view detailed descriptions of a specific task, you can use:

```
cap -e [task] # Example: cap -e deploy:cold
```

The default tasks are as follows (and can be run with **cap [task]**):

deploy
> Deploys your project. This calls both *update* and *restart*. Note that this will generally only work for applications that have already been deployed once. For a *cold* deploy,

you'll want to take a look at the *deploy:cold* task, which handles the cold start specifically.

deploy:check

Tests deployment dependencies. Checks things like directory permissions, necessary utilities, and so forth, reporting on the things that appear to be incorrect or missing. This is good for making sure a *deploy* has a chance of working before you actually run `cap deploy`.

deploy:cleanup

Cleans up old releases. By default, the last five releases are kept on each server (though you can change this with the `keep_releases` variable). All other deployed revisions are removed from the servers. By default, this will use `sudo` to clean up the old releases, but if sudo is not available for your environment, set the `:use_sudo` variable to `false` instead.

deploy:cold

Deploys and starts a *cold* application. This is useful if you have not deployed your application before or if your application is (for some other reason) not currently running. It will deploy the code, run any pending migrations, and then instead of invoking `'deploy:restart'`, it will invoke `'deploy:start'` to fire up the application servers.

deploy:migrate

Runs the migrate Rake task. By default, it runs this in the most recently deployed version of the app. However, you can specify a different release via the `migrate_target` variable, which must be one of `:latest` (for the default behavior) or `:current` (for the release indicated by the *current* symlink). Strings will work for those values instead of symbols too. You can also specify additional environment variables to pass to Rake via the `migrate_env` variable. Finally, you can specify the full path to the Rake executable by setting the Rake variable. The defaults are:

```
set :rake,            "rake"
set :rails_env,       "production"
set :migrate_env,     ""
set :migrate_target,  :latest
```

deploy:migrations

Deploys and runs pending migrations. This will work similarly to the *deploy* task but will also run any pending migrations (via the **deploy:migrate** task) prior to updating the symlink. The update in this case is not atomic, and transactions are not used, because migrations are not guaranteed to be reversible.

deploy:pending

Displays the commits since your last deploy. This is good for a summary of the changes that have occurred since the last deploy. This might not be supported on all SCMs.

deploy:pending:diff

Displays the *diff* since your last deploy. This is useful if you want to examine what changes are about to be deployed. This might not be supported on all SCMs.

deploy:restart

Restarts your application. This works by calling the *script/process/reaper* script under the current path.

By default, this will be invoked via **sudo** as the *app* user. If you wish to run it as a different user, set the **:runner** variable to that user. If you are in an environment where you can't use **sudo**, set the **:use_sudo** variable to **false**:

```
set :use_sudo, false
```

deploy:rollback

Rolls back to a previous version and restarts. This is handy if you ever discover that you've deployed a lemon; **cap rollback** and you're right back where you were, on the previously deployed version.

deploy:rollback_code

Rolls back to the previously deployed version. The *current* symlink will be updated to point at the previously deployed version, and then the current release will be removed from the servers. You'll generally want to call **roll back** instead, as it performs a *restart* as well.

deploy:setup

Prepares one or more servers for deployment. Before you can use any of the Capistrano deployment tasks with your project, you will need to make sure all of your servers have been prepared with `cap deploy:setup`. When you add a new server to your cluster, you can easily run the setup task on just that server by specifying the HOSTS environment variable:

```
cap HOSTS=new.server.com deploy:setup
```

It is safe to run this task on servers that have already been set up; it will not destroy any deployed revisions or data.

deploy:start

Starts the application servers. This will attempt to invoke a script in your application called *script/spin*, which must know how to start your application listeners. For Rails applications, you might just have that script invoke *script/process/spawner* with the appropriate arguments.

By default, the script will be executed via `sudo` as the *app* user. If you wish to run it as a different user, set the `:runner` variable to that user. If you are in an environment where you can't use `sudo`, set the `:use_sudo` variable to `false`.

deploy:stop

Stops the application servers. This will call *script/process/reaper* for the spawner process and all of the application processes it has spawned. As such, it is fairly Rails specific and may need to be overridden for other systems.

By default, the script will be executed via `sudo` as the *app* user. If you wish to run it as a different user, set the `:runner` variable to that user. If you are in an environment where you can't use `sudo`, set the `:use_sudo` variable to `false`.

deploy:symlink

Updates the symlink to the most recently deployed version. Capistrano works by putting each new release of your application in its own directory. When you deploy a new version, this task's job is to update the *current* symlink to point at the new version. You will rarely need to call this task directly; instead, use the *deploy* task (which performs a complete deploy, including *restart*) or the *update* task (which does everything except *restart*).

deploy:update

Copies your project and updates the symlink. It does this in a transaction, so that if either *update_code* or *symlink* fail, all changes made to the remote servers will be rolled back, leaving your system in the same state it was in before *update* was invoked. Usually, you will want to call *deploy* instead of *update*, but *update* can be handy if you want to deploy but not immediately restart your application.

deploy:update_code

Copies your project to the remote servers. This is the first stage of any deployment: moving your updated code and assets to the deployment servers. You will rarely call this task directly, however; instead, you should call the *deploy* task (to do a complete deploy) or the *update* task (if you want to perform the *restart* task separately).

You will need to make sure you set the :scm variable to the source control software you are using (it defaults to :subversion), and the :deploy_via variable to the strategy you want to use to deploy (it defaults to :checkout).

deploy:upload

Copies files to the currently deployed version. This is useful for updating files piecemeal, such as when you need to quickly deploy only a single file. Some files—such as updated templates, images, or stylesheets—might not require a full deploy, and especially in emergency situations, it can be handy to just push the updates to production quickly.

To use this task, specify the files and directories you want to copy as a comma-delimited list in the FILES environment variable. All directories will be processed recursively, with all files being pushed to the deployment servers. Any file or directory starting with a "." character will be ignored.

```
cap deploy:upload FILES=templates,controller.rb
```

deploy:web:disable

Presents a maintenance page to visitors. Disables your application's web interface by writing a *maintenance.html* file to each web server. The servers must be configured to detect the presence of this file and, if it is present, always display it instead of performing the request.

By default, the maintenance page will just say the site is down for "maintenance," and will be back "shortly," but you can customize the page by specifying the REASON and UNTIL environment variables:

```
cap deploy:web:disable \
    REASON="hardware upgrade" \
    UNTIL="12pm Central Time"
```

Further customization will require that you write your own task.

deploy:web:enable

Makes the application web-accessible again. Removes the *maintenance.html* page generated by deploy:web:disable, which (if your web servers are configured correctly) will make your application web-accessible again.

invoke

Invokes a single command on the remote servers. This is useful for performing one-off commands that may not require a full task to be written for them. Simply specify the command to execute via the COMMAND environment variable. To execute the command only on certain roles, specify the ROLES environment variable as a comma-delimited list of role names. Alternatively, you can specify the HOSTS environment variable as a comma-delimited list of hostnames to execute the task on those hosts explicitly. Lastly, if you want to execute the command via sudo, specify a nonempty value for the SUDO environment variable.

Sample usage:

```
cap COMMAND=uptime HOSTS=foo.capistrano.test invoke
cap ROLES=app,web SUDO=1 COMMAND="tail
  -f /var/log/messages"
  invoke
```

shell

Begins an interactive Capistrano session. This gives you an interactive terminal from which to execute tasks and commands on all of your servers.

CAUTION

shell is still an experimental feature, and is subject to change without notice!

For more information on setting up and using Capistrano with your Rails applications, go to *http://capify.org*.

TextMate

When developing Rails applications on a Mac, TextMate by MacroMates is by far the best choice (*http://macromates.com*). See Table 1-4 for some common shortcuts.

Table 1-4. TextMate shortcuts

Shortcut	Description	Shortcut	Description
⌘T	File menu	⌃\	Test runner menu
⇧⌘T	Method menu	⌥	Show fixture names for model
⌥⌘T	Bundle menu	⌘R, ⌘⇧R	Run test
⌃⇧|	Rails menu	def(t|tp)	Method or test method
⇧⌥⌘↓	Navigation menu	as(e|m|d|…)	Assertions
⌥⌘↓	Navigate	ft, ff, ffe	form_for
mcol	Create column in table	f.	Form element

Shortcut	Description	Shortcut	Description
`t.`	Create sexy column	⌃ ⇧ <	ERb tag
`hm, ho, hmt, bt`	Model associations	⌃ ⇧ H	Create partial from selection
`v(a｜u｜c｜p｜f｜ n｜e｜l｜i)`	Validations	`rp(c｜o｜s｜l)`	Render partial
⌃ ⇧ ⌘ S	Show schema	`li(p｜pp｜np｜ a｜c｜m｜…)`	link_to
`fina, finf, fini`	Model finders	⌫	Delete
⌃P	params[:id]	⌃	Control
`rest`	respond_to block	⌥	Option
`wants`	wants block	⌘	Command
`defcreat`	Create action	⇧	Shift
`rea`	Redirect		Escape
`rp(c｜o｜s｜l)`	Routes	↵	Return
⌘ ⇧ {	Toggle { } and do-end	⌅	Enter (fn+Return)

Helpers

Helpers or view helpers are modules that are available to use in your views. They provide shortcuts for commonly used code snippits. Here is a list of commonly used helpers and their methods.

ActiveRecordHelper

The ActiveRecordHelper makes it easier to create forms for records kept in instance variables.

The methods are described as follows.

error_message_on

```
error_message_on(object, method, prepend_text = "",
append_text = "", css_class = "formError")
```

Returns a string with a DIV containing all of the error messages for the objects located as instance variables by the names given.

Example

```
<%= error_message_on "post", "title" %>
# <div class="formError">can't be empty</div>

<%= error_message_on "post", "title", "Title simply ",
              " (or it won't work).", "inputError" %>
# <div class="inputError">Title simply can't be empty
  (or it won't work).</div>
```

error_messages_for

```
error_messages_for(*params)
```

Returns a string with a DIV containing all of the error messages for the objects located as instance variables by the names given.

This DIV can be tailored with the following options:

header_tag
> Used for the header of the error DIV (default: h2).

id
> The id of the error DIV (default: errorExplanation).

class
> The class of the error DIV (default: errorExplanation).

object
> The object (or array of objects) for which to display errors, if you need to escape the instance variable convention.

object_name
> The object name to use in the header, or any text that you prefer. If object_name is not set, the name of the first object will be used.

header_message
> The message in the header of the error DIV. Pass nil or an empty string to avoid the header message altogether (default: X errors prohibited this object from being saved).

message
> The explanation message after the header message and before the error list. Pass nil or an empty string to avoid the explanation message altogether. (default: There were problems with the following fields:).

Examples

```
error_messages_for 'user'
error_messages_for 'user_common', 'user', :object_name => 'user'
error_messages_for 'user', :object => @question.user
```

form

```
form(record_name, options = {}) {|contents if block_given?| ...}
```

Returns an entire form with all needed input tags for a specified Active Record object.

Example

Let's say you have the model Article with the attribute named title of type VARCHAR and body of type TEXT:

```
form("post")
```

This would result in:

```
<form action='/post/create' method='post'>
  <p>
    <label for="post_title">Title</label><br />
    <input id="post_title" name="post[title]" size="30" type="text"
    value="Hello World" />
  </p>
  <p>
    <label for="post_body">Body</label><br />
    <textarea cols="40" id="post_body" name="post[body]" rows="20">
    </textarea>
  </p>
  <input type='submit' value='Create' />
</form>
```

input

```
input(record_name, method, options = {})
```

Returns a default input tag for the type of object returned by the method.

Example

Let's say you have a model that has the attribute title of type VARCHAR column, and this instance holds "Hello World":

```
input("post", "title")
# <input id="post_title"  name="post[title]"
#  size="30" type="text" value="Hello World" />
```

AssetTagHelper

This module provides methods for generating HTML that links views to assets, such as images, javascripts, stylesheets, and feeds. These methods do not verify that assets exist before linking to them.

The methods are described as follows.

image_path

```
image_path(source)
```

Computes the path to an image asset in the public images directory. Full paths from the document root will be passed through. Used internally by image_tag to build the image path.

Examples

```
image_path("edit")            # => /images/edit
image_path("edit.png")        # => /images/edit.png
image_path("icons/edit.png")  # => /images/icons/edit.png
image_path("/icons/edit.png") # => /icons/edit.png
```

image_tag

```
image_tag(source, options = {})
```

Returns an HTML image tag for the source. The source can be a full path or a file that exists in your public images directory.

Options

:alt

> If no alt text is given, the filename part of the source is used (capitalized and without the extension).

:size

> Supplied as {Width}x{Height}, so 30x45 becomes width=30 and height=45. :size will be ignored if the value is not in the correct format.

:mouseover

> Sets an alternate image to be used when the onmouseover event is fired, and sets the original image to be replaced on-mouseout. This can be used to implement an easy image toggle that fires on onmouseover.

Examples

```
image_tag("icon")
# <img src="/images/icon" alt="Icon" />

image_tag("icon.png")
# <img src="/images/icon.png" alt="Icon" />

image_tag("icon.png", :size -> "16x10", :alt => "Edit Entry")
# <img src="/images/icon.png" width="16" height="10"
# alt="Edit Entry" />

image_tag("/icons/icon.gif", :size => "16x16")
# <img src="/icons/icon.gif" width="16" height="16"
# alt="Icon" />

image_tag("/icons/icon.gif", :height => '32', :width => '32')
# <img alt="Icon" height="32" src="/icons/icon.gif"
#   width="32" />

image_tag("/icons/icon.gif", :class => "menu_icon")
# <img alt="Icon" class="menu_icon" src="/icons/icon.gif" />

image_tag("mouse.png", :mouseover => "/images/mouse_over.png")
# <img src="/images/mouse.png"
```

```
# onmouseover="this.src='/images/mouse_over.png'"
# onmouseout="this.src='/images/mouse.png'" alt="Mouse" />

image_tag("mouse.png", :mouseover => image_path("mouse_over.png"))
# <img src="/images/mouse.png"
# onmouseover="this.src='/images/mouse_over.png'"
# onmouseout="this.src='/images/mouse.png'" alt="Mouse" />
```

javascript_include_tag

```
javascript_include_tag(*sources)
```

Returns an HTML script tag for each of the sources provided.

Examples

```
javascript_include_tag "xmlhr"
# <script type="text/javascript" src="/javascripts/xmlhr.js"></script>

javascript_include_tag "xmlhr.js"
# <script type="text/javascript" src="/javascripts/xmlhr.js"></script>

javascript_include_tag "common.javascript", "/elsewhere/cools"
# <script type="text/javascript"
#         src="/javascripts/common.javascript"></script>
# <script type="text/javascript" src="/elsewhere/cools.js"></script>

javascript_include_tag "http://www.railsapplication.com/xmlhr"
# <script type="text/javascript"
#          src="http://www.railsapplication.com/xmlhr.js"></script>

javascript_include_tag "http://www.railsapplication.com/xmlhr.js"
# <script type="text/javascript"
#          src="http://www.railsapplication.com/xmlhr.js"></script>

javascript_include_tag :defaults
# <script type="text/javascript"
#         src="/javascripts/prototype.js"></script>
# <script type="text/javascript"
#         src="/javascripts/effects.js"></script>
# ...
# <script type="text/javascript"
#         src="/javascripts/application.js"></script>
```

stylesheet_link_tag

stylesheet_link_tag(*sources*)

Returns a stylesheet link tag for the sources specified as arguments. If you don't specify an extension, *.css* will be appended automatically. You can modify the link attributes by passing a hash as the last argument.

Examples

```
stylesheet_link_tag "style"
# <link href="/stylesheets/style.css"
#       media="screen" rel="stylesheet" type="text/css" />

stylesheet_link_tag "style.css"
# <link href="/stylesheets/style.css"
#       media="screen" rel="stylesheet" type="text/css" />

stylesheet_link_tag "http://www.railsapplication.com/style.css"
# <link href="http://www.railsapplication.com/style.css"
#       media="screen" rel="stylesheet" type="text/css" />

stylesheet_link_tag "style", :media => "all"
# <link href="/stylesheets/style.css"
#       media="all" rel="stylesheet" type="text/css" />

stylesheet_link_tag "style", :media => "print"
# <link href="/stylesheets/style.css"
#       media="print" rel="stylesheet" type="text/css" />

stylesheet_link_tag "random.styles", "/css/stylish"
# <link href="/stylesheets/random.styles"
#       media="screen" rel="stylesheet" type="text/css" />
# <link href="/css/stylish.css"
        media="screen" rel="stylesheet" type="text/css" />
```

CacheHelper

This helper exposes a method for the caching of view fragments.

The method is described below.

cache

```
cache(name = {}, &block)
```

A method for caching fragments of a view rather than an entire action or page. This technique is useful for caching pieces like menus, lists of news topics, static HTML fragments, and so on. This method takes a block that contains the content you wish to cache.

Examples

```
# Cache a partial
<% cache do %>
  <%= render :partial => "menu" %>
<% end %>

# Cache static content
<% cache do %>
  <p>Hello users!  Welcome to our website!</p>
<% end %>

# Cache static content mixed with dynamic content
<% cache do %>
  Topics:
  <%= render :partial => "topics", :collection => @topic_list %>
  <i>Topics listed alphabetically</i>
<% end %>
```

DateHelper

The DateHelper primarily creates select/option tags for different kinds of dates and date elements. All of the select-type methods share a number of common options that are as follows:

:prefix

> Overwrites the default prefix of "date" used for the select names. So specifying "birthday" would give birthday[month] instead of date[month] if passed to the select_month method.

:include_blank

> Set to true if it should be possible to set an empty date.

:discard_type

> Set to true if you want to discard the type part of the select name. If set to true, the select_month method would use simply "date" (which can be overwritten using :prefix) instead of "date[month]".

The DateHelper methods are described below.

---

datetime_select

datetime_select(*object_name, method, options = {}*)

Returns a set of select tags (one for year, month, day, hour, and minute) preselected for accessing a specified datetime-based attribute (identified by method) on an object assigned to the template (identified by object).

Examples

```
# Generates a datetime select that, when POSTed, will be stored
# in the post variable in the written_on attribute
datetime_select("post", "written_on")

# Generates a datetime select with a year select that starts at 1995
# that, when POSTed, will be stored in the post variable in the
# written_on attribute.
datetime_select("post", "written_on", :start_year => 1995)

# Generates a datetime select with a default value of 3 days
# from the current time that, when POSTed, will be stored
# in the trip variable in the departing attribute.
datetime_select("trip", "departing", :default => 3.days.from_now)

# Generates a datetime select that discards the type that, when POSTed,
# will be stored in the post variable as the written_on attribute.
datetime_select("post", "written_on", :discard_type => true)
```

distance_of_time_in_words

```
distance_of_time_in_words(from_time, to_time = 0,
include_seconds = false)
```

Reports as seconds the approximate distance in time between two Time or Date objects or integers.

Examples

```
from_time = Time.now
distance_of_time_in_words(from_time, from_time + 50.minutes)
# about 1 hour
distance_of_time_in_words(from_time, 50.minutes.from_now)
# about 1 hour
distance_of_time_in_words(from_time, from_time + 15.seconds)
# less than a minute
distance_of_time_in_words(from_time, from_time + 15.seconds, true)
# less than 20 seconds
distance_of_time_in_words(from_time, 3.years.from_now)
# over 3 years
distance_of_time_in_words(from_time, from_time + 60.hours)
# about 3 days
distance_of_time_in_words(from_time, from_time + 45.seconds, true)
# less than a minute
distance_of_time_in_words(from_time, from_time - 45.seconds, true)
# less than a minute
distance_of_time_in_words(from_time, 76.seconds.from_now)
# 1 minute
distance_of_time_in_words(from_time, from_time + 1.year + 3.days)
# about 1 year

to_time = Time.now + 6.years + 19.days
distance_of_time_in_words(from_time, to_time, true)
# over 6 years
distance_of_time_in_words(to_time, from_time, true)
# over 6 years
distance_of_time_in_words(Time.now, Time.now)
# less than a minute
```

select_date

```
select_date(date = Date.today, options = {})
```

Returns a set of HTML select tags (one for year, month, and day) preselected with the date. It's possible to explicitly set the order of the tags using the :order option with an array of symbols

for :year, :month, and :day in the desired order. If you do not
supply a symbol, it will be appended onto the :order passed in.

Examples

```
my_date = Time.today + 6.days

# Generates a date select that defaults to the date in my_date
# (six days after today)
select_date(my_date)

# Generates a date select that defaults to today
select_date()

# Generates a date select that defaults to the date in my_date
# (six days after today) with the fields ordered year, month,
# day rather than month, day, year.
select_date(my_date, :order => [:year, :month, :day])

# Generates a date select that discards the type of the field
# and defaults to the date in my_date (six days after today)
select_datetime(my_date time, :discard_type => true)

# Generates a date select that defaults to the datetime in
# my_date (six days after today) prefixed with 'payday'
# rather than 'date'.
select_datetime(my_date_time, :prefix => 'payday')
```

select_datetime

```
select_datetime(datetime = Time.now, options = {})
```

Returns a set of HTML select tags (one for year, month, day,
hour, and minute) preselected with the datetime. It's also possible to explicitly set the order of the tags using the :order option
with an array of symbols for :year, :month, and :day in the desired order. If you do not supply a symbol, it will be appended
onto the :order passed in. You can also add :date_separator
and :time_separator keys to the options to control visual display
of the elements.

Examples

```
my_date_time = Time.now + 4.days

# Generates a datetime select that defaults to the datetime
# in my_date_time (four days after today)
select_datetime(my_date_time)
```

```
# Generates a datetime select that defaults to today
# (no specified datetime)
select_datetime()

# Generates a datetime select that defaults to the datetime
# in my_date_time (four days after today) with the fields
# ordered year, month, day rather than month, day, year.
select_datetime(my_date_time, :order => [:year, :month, :day])

# Generates a datetime select that defaults to the datetime in
# my_date_time (four days after today) with a '/' between each
# date field.
select_datetime(my_date_time, :date_separator => '/')

# Generates a datetime select that discards the type of the
# field and defaults to the datetime in my_date_time (four
# days after today)
select_datetime(my_date_time, :discard_type => true)

# Generates a datetime select that defaults to the datetime in
# my_date_time (four days after today) prefixed with 'payday'
# rather than 'date'.
select_datetime(my_date_time, :prefix => 'payday')
```

select_day

```
select_day(date, options = {})
```

Returns a select tag with options for each of the days 1 through 31 with the current day selected. The date can also be substituted for an hour number. Override the field name using the :field_name option, 'day', by default.

Examples

```
my_date = Time.today + 2.days

# Generates a select field for days that defaults to the day for
# the date in my_date
select_day(my_time)

# Generates a select field for days that defaults to the number
# given
select_day(5)

# Generates a select field for days that defaults to the day
# for the date in my_date that is named 'due' rather than 'day'
select_day(my_time, :field_name => 'due')
```

select_hour

```
select_hour(datetime, options = {})
```

Returns a select tag with options for each of the hours 0 through 23 with the current hour selected. The hour can also be substituted for a hour number. Override the field name using the :field_name option, 'hour', by default.

Examples

```
my_time = Time.now + 6.hours

# Generates a select field for minutes that defaults to the minutes
# for the time in my_time
select_minute(my_time)

# Generates a select field for minutes that defaults to the
# number given
select_minute(14)

# Generates a select field for minutes that defaults to the minutes
# for the time in my_time that is named 'stride' rather than 'second'.
select_minute(my_time, :field_name => 'stride')
```

select_minute

```
select_minute(datetime, options = {})
```

Returns a select tag with options for each of the minutes 0 through 59 with the current minute selected. Also can return a select tag with options by minute_step from 0 through 59 with the 00 minute selected. The minute can also be substituted for a minute number. Override the field name using the :field_name option, 'minute', by default.

Examples

```
my_time = Time.now + 6.hours

# Generates a select field for minutes that defaults to
# the minutes for the time in my_time
select_minute(my_time)

# Generates a select field for minutes that defaults to
# the number given
select_minute(14)
```

```
# Generates a select field for minutes that defaults to the minutes
# for the time in my_time that is named 'stride' rather than 'second'
select_minute(my_time, :field_name => 'stride')
```

select_month

```
select_month(date, options = {})
```

Returns a select tag with options for each of the months January through December with the current month selected.

Examples

```
# Generates a select field for months that defaults to the current
# month that will use keys like "January", "March".
select_month(Date.today)

# Generates a select field for months that defaults to the current
# month that is named "start" rather than "month"
select_month(Date.today, :field_name => 'start')

# Generates a select field for months that defaults to the current
# month that will use keys like "1", "3".
select_month(Date.today, :use_month_numbers => true)

# Generates a select field for months that defaults to the current
# month that will use keys like "1 - January", "3 - March".
select_month(Date.today, :add_month_numbers => true)

# Generates a select field for months that defaults to the current
# month that will use keys like "Jan", "Mar".
select_month(Date.today, :use_short_month => true)

# Generates a select field for months that defaults to the current
# month that will use keys like "Januar", "Marts."
select_month(Date.today, :use_month_names => %w(Januar Februar Marts
...))
```

select_second

```
select_second(datetime, options = {})
```

Returns a select tag with options for each of the seconds 0 through 59 with the current second selected. The second can also be substituted for a second number. Override the field name using the :field_name option, 'second', by default.

Examples

```
my_time = Time.now + 16.minutes

# Generates a select field for seconds that defaults to the seconds
# for the time in my_time
select_second(my_time)

# Generates a select field for seconds that defaults to the number
# given
select_second(33)

# Generates a select field for seconds that defaults to the seconds
# for the time in my_time that is named 'interval' rather than
# 'second'
select_second(my_time, :field_name => 'interval')
```

select_year

```
select_year(date, options = {})
```

Returns a select tag with options for each of the five years on each side of the current, which is selected.

Examples

```
# Generates a select field for years that defaults to the current
# year that has ascending year values
select_year(Date.today, :start_year => 1992, :end_year => 2007)

# Generates a select field for years that defaults to the current
# year that is named 'birth' rather than 'year'
select_year(Date.today, :field_name => 'birth')

# Generates a select field for years that defaults to the current
# year that has descending year values
select_year(Date.today, :start_year => 2005, :end_year => 1900)

# Generates a select field for years that defaults to the year
# 2008 that has ascending year values
select_year(2008, :start_year => 2000, :end_year => 2010)
```

time_select

```
time_select(object_name, method, options = {})
```

Returns a set of select tags (one for hour, minute, and optionally second) preselected for accessing a specified time-based attribute (identified by method) on an object assigned to the template (identified by object). You can include the seconds with :include_seconds.

Examples

```
# Creates a time select tag that, when POSTed, will be stored in
# the post variable in  the sunrise attribute
time_select("post", "sunrise")

# Creates a time select tag that, when POSTed, will be stored in
# the order variable in the submitted attribute
time_select("order", "submitted")

# Creates a time select tag that, when POSTed, will be stored in
# the mail variable in the sent_at attribute
time_select("mail", "sent_at")

# Creates a time select tag with a seconds field that, when POSTed,
# will be stored in the post variables in the sunrise attribute.
time_select("post", "start_time", :include_seconds => true)

# Creates a time select tag with a seconds field that, when POSTed,
# will be stored in  the entry variables in the submission_time
# attribute.
time_select("entry", "submission_time", :include_seconds => true)

# You can set the :minute_step to 15 which will give you:
# 00, 15, 30 and 45.
time_select 'game', 'game_time', {:minute_step => 15}
```

FormHelper

FormHelpers are designed to make working with models much easier (compared to using just standard HTML elements) by providing a set of methods for creating forms based on your models. This helper generates the HTML for forms, providing a method for each sort of input (e.g., text, password, select, and so on).

The methods are described below.

check_box

```
check_box(object_name, method, options = {},
checked_value = "1", unchecked_value = "0")
```

Returns a checkbox tag tailored for accessing a specified attribute (identified by method) on an object assigned to the template (identified by object).

Examples

```
# Let's say that @post.validated? is 1:
check_box("post", "validated")
# <input type="checkbox" id="post_validate"
#   name="post[validated]" value="1" checked="checked" />
# <input name="post[validated]" type="hidden" value="0" />

# Let's say that @puppy.gooddog is "no":
check_box("puppy", "gooddog", {}, "yes", "no")
# <input type="checkbox" id="puppy_gooddog"
#   name="puppy[gooddog]" value="yes" />
# <input name="puppy[gooddog]" type="hidden" value="no" />

check_box("eula", "accepted", {}, "yes", "no", :class => 'eula_check')
# <input type="checkbox" id="eula_accepted"
#   name="eula[accepted]" value="no" />
# <input name="eula[accepted]" type="hidden" value="no" />
```

fields_for

```
fields_for(record_or_name_or_array, *args)
{|builder.new(object_name, object, self, options, block)| ...}
```

Creates a scope around a specific model object, like form_for, but doesn't create the form tags themselves. This makes fields_for suitable for specifying additional model objects in the same form.

Examples

```
<% form_for @person, :url => { :action => "update" } do |person_form| %>
  First name: <%= person_form.text_field :first_name %>
  Last name : <%= person_form.text_field :last_name %>

  <% fields_for @person.permission do |permission_fields| %>
    Admin?  : <%= permission_fields.check_box :admin %>
  <% end %>
<% end %>
```

Alternatively, if you have an object that needs to be represented as a different parameter, like a Client that acts as a Person:

```
<% fields_for :person, @client do |permission_fields| %>
  Admin?: <%= permission_fields.check_box :admin %>
<% end %>
```

If you don't have an object, just a name of the parameter:

```
<% fields_for :person do |permission_fields| %>
  Admin?: <%= permission_fields.check_box :admin %>
<% end %>
```

file_field

```
file_field(object_name, method, options = {})
```

Returns a file upload input tag tailored for accessing a specified attribute (identified by method) on an object assigned to the template (identified by object). Additional options on the input tag can be passed as a hash with options. These options will be tagged onto the HTML as an HTML element attribute, as in the examples shown.

Examples

```
file_field(:user, :avatar)
# <input type="file" id="user_avatar" name="user[avatar]" />

file_field(:post, :attached, :accept => 'text/html')
# <input type="file" id="post_attached" name="post[attached]" />

file_field(:attachment, :file, :class => 'file_input')
# <input type="file" id="attachment_file" name="attachment[file]"
# class="file_input" />
```

form_for

```
form_for(record_or_name_or_array, *args, &proc)
```

Creates a form and a scope around a specific model object that is used as a base for questioning values for the fields.

Examples

```
<% form_for :person, @person, :url => { :action => "update" } do |f| %>
  First name: <%= f.text_field :first_name %>
```

```
  Last name : <%= f.text_field :last_name %>
  Biography : <%= f.text_area :biography %>
  Admin?    : <%= f.check_box :admin %>
<% end %>
```

Alternatively, if being used within a RESTful application:

```
<% form_for @person do |f| %>
  First name: <%= f.text_field :first_name %>
  Last name : <%= f.text_field :last_name %>
  Biography : <%= f.text_area :biography %>
  Admin?    : <%= f.check_box :admin %>
<% end %>
```

hidden_field

hidden_field(*object_name*, *method*, *options* = {})

Returns a hidden input tag tailored for accessing a specified attribute (identified by method) on an object assigned to the template (identified by object).

Example

```
hidden_field(:user, :token)
# <input type="hidden" id="user_token" name="user[token]"
#   value="#{@user.token}" />
```

label

label(*object_name*, *method*, *text* = nil, *options* = {})

Returns a label tag tailored for labelling an input field for a specified attribute (identified by method) on an object assigned to the template (identified by object).

Examples

```
label(:post, :title)
# <label for="post_title">Title</label>

label(:post, :title, "A short title")
# <label for="post_title">A short title</label>

label(:post, :title, "A short title", :class => "title_label")
# <label for="post_title" class="title_label">A short title</label>
```

password_field

```
password_field(object_name, method, options = {})
```

Returns an input tag of the "password" type tailored for accessing a specified attribute (identified by method) on an object assigned to the template (identified by object).

Examples

```
password_field(:login, :pass, :size => 20)
# <input type="text" id="login_pass" name="login[pass]"
#   size="20" value="#{@login.pass}" />

password_field(:account, :secret, :class => "form_input")
# <input type="text" id="account_secret" name="account[secret]"
# value="#{@account.secret}"  class="form_input" />

password_field(:user, :password,
    :onchange => "if $('user[password]').length > 30 {
                  alert('Your password needs to be shorter!'); }")
# <input type="text" id="user_password" name="user[password]"
# value="#{@user.password}" onchange = "if $('user[password]').length >
# 30 { alert('Your password needs to be shorter!'); }"/>

password_field(:account, :pin, :size => 20, :class => 'form_input')
# <input type="text" id="account_pin" name="account[pin]" size="20"
# value="#{@account.pin}" class="form_input" />
```

radio_button

```
radio_button(object_name, method, tag_value, options = {})
```

Returns a radio button tag for accessing a specified attribute (identified by method) on an object assigned to the template (identified by object).

Examples

```
# Let's say that @post.category returns "rails":
radio_button("post", "category", "rails")
# <input type="radio" id="post_category"
#         name="post[category]" value="rails"
#         checked="checked" />

radio_button("post", "category", "java")
# <input type="radio" id="post_category"
#         name="post[category]" value="java" />
```

```
radio_button("user", "receive_newsletter", "yes")
# <input type="radio" id="user_receive_newsletter"
#        name="user[receive_newsletter]" value="yes" />

radio_button("user", "receive_newsletter", "no")
# <input type="radio" id="user_receive_newsletter"
#        name="user[receive_newsletter]" value="no"
#        checked="checked" />
```

text_area

```
text_area(object_name, method, options = {})
```

Returns a text area opening and closing tag set tailored for accessing a specified attribute (identified by method) on an object assigned to the template (identified by object).

Examples

```
text_area(:post, :body, :cols => 20, :rows => 40)
# <textarea cols="20" rows="40" id="post_body"
#    name="post[body]"> {@post.body} </textarea>

text_area(:comment, :text, :size => "20x30")
# <textarea cols="20" rows="30" id="comment_text"
#    name="comment[text]"> {@comment.text} # </textarea>

text_area(:application, :notes, :cols => 40, :rows => 15,
          :class => 'app_input')
# <textarea cols="40" rows="15" id="application_notes"
#    name="application[notes]" class="app_input">
#    #{@application.notes} </textarea>

text_area(:entry, :body, :size => "20x20",
          :disabled => 'disabled')
# <textarea cols="20" rows="20" id="entry_body"
#    name="entry[body]" disabled="disabled">
#    #{@entry.body} </textarea>
```

text_field

```
text_field(object_name, method, options = {})
```

Returns an input tag of the "text" type tailored for accessing a specified attribute (identified by method) on an object assigned to the template (identified by object).

Examples

```
text_field(:post, :title, :size => 20)
# <input type="text" id="post_title" name="post[title]" size="20"
#   value="#{@post.title}" />

text_field(:post, :title, :class => "create_input")
# <input type="text" id="post_title" name="post[title]"
#   value="#{@post.title}" class="create_input" />

text_field(:session, :user,
           :onchange => "if $('session[user]').value   == 'admin'
                 { alert('Your login can not be admin!'); }")
# <input type="text" id="session_user" name="session[user]"
#   value="#{@session.user}" onchange = "if $('session[user]').value
#   == 'admin' { alert('Your login can not be admin!'); }"/>

text_field(:snippet, :code, :size => 20, :class => 'code_input')
# <input type="text" id="snippet_code" name="snippet[code]"
#   size="20" value="#{@snippet.code}" class="code_input" />
```

FormOptionsHelper

Provides a number of methods for turning different kinds of
containers into a set of option tags.

The methods are described below.

collection_select

```
collection_select(object, method, collection, value_method,
text_method, options = {}, html_options = {})
```

Returns a string of option tags for pretty much any country in
the world. Supply a country name as selected to have it marked
as the selected option tag. You can also supply an array of coun-
tries as priority_countries so that they will be listed above the
rest of the (long) list.

Examples

Example object structure for use with this method:

```
class Post < ActiveRecord::Base
  belongs_to :author
end
class Author < ActiveRecord::Base
  has_many :posts
```

```
def name_with_initial
  "#{first_name.first}. #{last_name}"
end
end
```

Sample usage (selecting the associated Author for an instance of Post, @post):

```
collection_select(:post, :author_id, Author.find(:all), :id,
                  :name_with_initial, {:prompt => true})
```

If @post.author_id is already 1, this would return:

```
<select name="post[author_id]">
  <option value="">Please select</option>
  <option value="1" selected="selected">D. Heinemeier Hansson</option>
  <option value="2">D. Thomas</option>
  <option value="3">M. Clark</option>
</select>
```

country_options_for_select

```
country_options_for_select(selected = nil,
priority_countries = nil)
```

Returns <select> and <option> tags for the collection of existing return values of method for object's class. The value returned from calling method on the instance object will be selected. If calling method returns nil, no selection is made without including :prompt or :include_blank in the options hash.

The :value_method and :text_method parameters are methods to be called on each member of the collection. The return values are used as the value attribute and contents of each <option> tag, respectively.

country_select

```
country_select(object, method, priority_countries = nil,
options = {}, html_options = {})
```

Returns select and option tags for the given object and method, using country_options_for_select to generate the list of option tags.

option_groups_from_collection_for_select

option_groups_from_collection_for_select(*collection,*
group_method, group_label_method, option_key_method,
option_value_method, elected_key = nil)

Returns a string of <option> tags, like options_from_collec
tion_for_select, but groups them by <optgroup> tags based on
the object relationships of the arguments.

Parameters

collection

An array of objects representing the <optgroup> tags.

group_method

The name of a method which, when called on a member of the
collection, returns an array of child objects representing the
<option> tags.

group_label_method

The name of a method which, when called on a member of the
collection, returns a string to be used as the label attribute for
its <optgroup> tag.

option_key_method

The name of a method which, when called on a child object
of a member of the collection, returns a value to be used as the
value attribute for its <option> tag.

option_value_method

The name of a method which, when called on a child object
of a member of the collection, returns a value to be used as the
contents of its <option> tag.

selected_key

A value equal to the value attribute for one of the <option>
tags, which will have the selected attribute set. Corresponds
to the return value of one of the calls to option_key_method. If
nil, no selection is made.

Examples

Example objects for use with this method:

```
class Continent < ActiveRecord::Base
  has_many :countries
  # attribs: id, name
end
class Country < ActiveRecord::Base
  belongs_to :continent
  # attribs: id, name, continent_id
end
```

Sample usage:

```
option_groups_from_collection_for_select(@continents, :countries,
  :name, :id, :name, 3)
```

Possible output:

```
<optgroup label="Africa">
  <option value="1">Egypt</option>
  <option value="4">Rwanda</option>
  ...
</optgroup>
<optgroup label="Asia">
  <option value="3" selected="selected">China</option>
  <option value="12">India</option>
  <option value="5">Japan</option>
  ...
</optgroup>
```

options_for_select

```
options_for_select(container, selected = nil)
```

Accepts a container (hash, array, enumerable, your type) and
returns a string of option tags. Given a container where the elements respond to first and last (such as a two-element array),
the "lasts" serve as option values and the "firsts" as option text.
Hashes are turned into this form automatically, so the keys become "firsts" and values become "lasts." If selected is specified,
the matching "last" or element will get the selected option tag.
An array of values may also be selected when using a multiple
select.

Examples

```
options_for_select([["Dollar", "$"], ["Kroner", "DKK"]])
# <option value="$">Dollar</option>
# <option value="DKK">Kroner</option>

options_for_select([ "VISA", "MasterCard" ], "MasterCard")
```

```
# <option>VISA</option>
# <option selected="selected">MasterCard</option>

options_for_select({ "Basic" => "$20", "Plus" => "$40" }, "$40")
# <option value="$20">Basic</option>
# <option value="$40" selected="selected">Plus</option>

options_for_select([ "VISA", "MasterCard", "Discover" ], ["VISA", "Discover"])
# <option selected="selected">VISA</option>
# <option>MasterCard</option>
# <option selected="selected">Discover</option>
```

options_from_collection_for_select

Synopsis

```
options_from_collection_for_select(collection,
value_method, text_method, selected = nil)
```

Returns a string of option tags that have been compiled by iterating the collection and assigning the result of a call to the value_method as the option value and the text_method as the option text. If selected is specified, the element returning a match on value_method will get the selected option tag.

Examples

```
options_from_collection_for_select(@project.people, "id", "name")
# <option value="#{person.id}">#{person.name}</option>
```

select

Synopsis

```
select(object, method, choices, options = {}, html_options = {})
```

Creates a select tag and a series of contained option tags for the provided object and method. The option currently held by the object will be selected, provided that the object is available. See options_for_select for the required format of the choices parameter.

Examples

Example with @post.person_id => 1:

```
select("post", "person_id", Person.find(:all).collect {|p|
[ p.name, p.id ] },
      { :include_blank => true })
```

This could become:

```
<select name="post[person_id]">
  <option value=""></option>
  <option value="1" selected="selected">David</option>
  <option value="2">Sam</option>
  <option value="3">Tobias</option>
</select>
```

NumberHelper

The NumberHelper provides methods for converting numbers into formatted strings. Methods are provided for phone numbers, currency, percentage, precision, positional notation, and file size.

The methods are described below.

number_to_currency

```
number_to_currency(number, options = {})
```

Formats a number into a currency string (e.g., $13.65). You can customize the format in the options hash.

Options

:precision
> Sets the level of precision (defaults to 2)

:unit
> Sets the denomination of the currency (defaults to "$")

:separator
> Sets the separator between the units (defaults to ".")

:delimiter
> Sets the thousands delimiter (defaults to ",")

Examples

```
number_to_currency(1234567890.50)
# => $1,234,567,890.50
```

```
number_to_currency(1234567890.506)
# => $1,234,567,890.51
number_to_currency(1234567890.506, :precision => 3)
# => $1,234,567,890.506
```

number_to_human_size

```
number_to_human_size(size, precision=1)
```

Formats the bytes in size into a more understandable representation (e.g., giving it 1500 yields 1.5 KB). This method is useful
for reporting file sizes to users.

Examples

```
number_to_human_size(123)            # => 123 Bytes
number_to_human_size(1234)           # => 1.2 KB
number_to_human_size(12345)          # => 12.1 KB
number_to_human_size(1234567)        # => 1.2 MB
number_to_human_size(1234567890)     # => 1.1 GB
number_to_human_size(1234567890123)  # => 1.1 TB
number_to_human_size(1234567, 2)     # => 1.18 MB
number_to_human_size(483989, 0)      # => 4 MB
```

number_to_percentage

```
number_to_percentage(number, options = {})
```

Formats a number as a percentage string (e.g., 65%). You can
customize the format in the options hash.

Options

:precision
    Sets the level of precision (defaults to 2)

:separator
    Sets the separator between the units (defaults to ".")

Examples

```
number_to_percentage(100)                              # => 100.000%
number_to_percentage(100, :precision => 0)             # => 100%

number_to_percentage(302.24398923423, :precision => 5) # => 302.24399%
```

number_to_phone

number_with_precision(*number, precision=3*)

Formats a number with the specified level of precision (e.g., 112.32 has a precision of 2). The default level of precision is 3.

Options

:area_code
> Adds parentheses around the area code

:delimiter
> Specifies the delimiter to use (defaults to "-")

:extension
> Specifies an extension to add to the end of the generated number

:country_code
> Sets the country code for the phone number

Examples

```
number_to_phone(1235551234)
# => 123-555-1234
number_to_phone(1235551234, :area_code => true)
# => (123) 555-1234
number_to_phone(1235551234, :delimiter => " ")
# => 123 555 1234
number_to_phone(1235551234, :area_code => true, :extension => 5)
# => (123) 555-1234 x 5
number_to_phone(1235551234, :country_code => 1)
# => +1-123-555-1234
```

number_with_delimiter

number_with_delimiter(*number, delimiter=",", separator="."*)

Formats a number with grouped thousands using *delimiter* (e.g., 12,324). You can customize the format using optional delimiter and separator parameters.

Options

:delimiter
>   Specifies the delimiter to use (defaults to ",")

:separator
>   Sets the separator between the units (defaults to ".")

Examples

```
number_with_delimiter(12345678)                # => 12,345,678
number_with_delimiter(12345678.05)             # => 12,345,678.05
number_with_delimiter(12345678, ".")           # => 12.345.678

number_with_delimiter(98765432.98, " ", ",")   # => 98 765 432,98
```

number_with_precision

```
number_with_delimiter(number, delimiter=",", separator=".")
```

Formats a number with the specified level of precision (e.g., 112.32 has a precision of 2). The default level of precision is 3.

Examples

```
number_with_precision(111.2345)     # => 111.235
number_with_precision(111.2345, 2)  # => 111.24
number_with_precision(13, 5)        # => 13.00000
number_with_precision(389.32314, 0) # => 389
```

Index

We'd like to hear your suggestions for improving our indexes. Send email to
index@oreilly.com.

X

Y